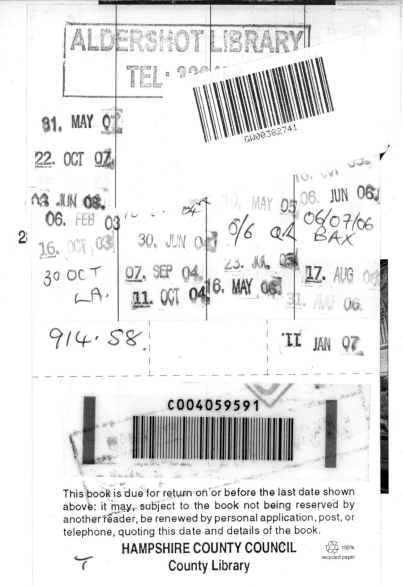

This book is due for return on or before the last date shown above: it may, subject to the book not being reserved by another reader, be renewed by personal application, post, or telephone, quoting this date and details of the book.

HAMPSHIRE COUNTY COUNCIL
County Library

100% recycled paper

NEW HOLLAND

NEW HOLLAND

★★★ Highly recommended
★★ Recommended
★ See if you can

First edition published in 2002
by New Holland Publishers (UK) Ltd
London • Cape Town • Sydney • Auckland
10 9 8 7 6 5 4 3 2 1

website: www.newhollandpublishers.com

Garfield House, 86 Edgware Road
London W2 2EA
United Kingdom

80 McKenzie Street
Cape Town 8001
South Africa

14 Aquatic Drive
Frenchs Forest, NSW 2086
Australia

218 Lake Road
Northcote, Auckland
New Zealand

Distributed in the USA by
The Globe Pequot Press
Connecticut

ISBN 1 84330 042 7

Publishing Manager: John Loubser
Managing Editor: Thea Grobbelaar
DTP Cartographic Manager: Genené Hart

Editor: Jacqueline de Villiers
Design and DTP: Éloïse Moss, Lellyn Creamer
Cartographer: Nicole Engeler
Consultant: Tracey Gambarotta
Picture Researcher: Colleen Abrahams
Proofreader: Thea Grobbelaar
Reproduction by Hirt & Carter (Pty) Ltd, Cape Town
Printed and bound in Hong Kong by Sing Cheong
Printing Co. Ltd.

Acknowledgements:
The author would like to thank the following people
for their assistance in researching this book: Sara
Louise Harper, Doriana Calajò (AAPIT Palermo),
Dr Giulio Bartoli, and especially Judith Chatfield
for her art historical scholarship, willing assistance
and fine company during research in Sicily.

Photographic Credits:
Mark Azavedo: pages 26, 39, 69;
Sylvia Cordaiy PL/Gable: page 10;
Sylvia Cordaiy PL/Eve Miessler: page 106;
Gallo/Tony Stone Images/Simeene Huber: page 8;
Gallo/Tony Stone Images/Gary Yeowell: page 110;
Paul Harris: pages 30, 36, 66;
Image-Link: cover, title page, pages 4, 6, 7, 9, 11, 12,
13, 14, 15, 16, 18, 19, 20, 21, 22, 24, 25, 27, 28, 29, 32, 33,
35, 38, 40, 41, 42, 43, 44, 46, 49, 52, 57, 58, 60, 62, 63, 71,
72, 74, 75, 76, 77, 78, 79, 80, 81, 84, 86, 87, 88a, 88b, 89,
90, 91, 92, 95, 96, 97, 100, 103, 104, 105, 107, 111, 112,
113, 114, 116, 117, 118, 119;
PhotoBank/Peter Baker: page 23;
Jeroen Snijders: pages 34, 37, 45, 47, 54, 56, 59, 61, 70,
73, 93, 109.

Although every effort has been made to ensure
accuracy of facts, and telephone and fax numbers
in this book, the publishers will not be held
responsible for changes that occur at the time of
going to press.

Cover: *One of Sicily's most impressive sights, the Doric
temple at Segesta is also one of the Classical World's best
preserved monuments.*
Title Page: *Catania's ornate Duomo is a fine renovated
Renaissance and Baroque building.*

CONTENTS

1
Introducing Sicily

The Phoenicians, Greeks, Romans and Moors, not to mention the Spanish, French and English, have for over three millennia recognized the strategic importance of Sicily and claimed it, at various times, as their own. A Mediterranean island, Sicily embraced and absorbed both the African and European cultures passing through it and created an identity of her own. Exploring this unique microcosm is fascinating and inspiring.

While the politics of the Mediterranean shaped the culture of the islanders, it was – and still is – snow-capped Mount Etna, the island's dangerously volatile volcano, which has defined Sicily's profile. As both creator and destroyer, its eruptions and earthquakes have fashioned the physiognomy of eastern Sicily just as the small volcanoes on the starkly beautiful Aeolian islands, to the north of Sicily, have contributed to their emergence and destruction. Mount Etna has wiped out Sicilian villages yet, at the same time, it has provided a rich agricultural land.

The Sicily of today is a magical blend of classical antiquity, Arabic elegance, European culture, Italian style and savage beauty. It is populated by shy, yet tough, sincere people who have learned to adapt to change and survive. Proud and sometimes defiant, the Sicilians welcome visitors to their shores, to share their heritage and to marvel at its beauty. But their sights are always set higher – on the brooding form of Mount Etna. It is she, and not the politicians, who shapes the island's destiny.

TOP ATTRACTIONS

*** Roman Villa Casale: a fabulous private villa with magnificent mosaics.
*** Taormina: Attend a performance on the steps of the Greek theatre (June–August).
*** Segesta: a fine temple in a pastoral landscape.
*** Monreale: a glittering interpretation of the Bible in mosaic.
*** Stromboli: active volcano best viewed by night.
** Ragusa Ibla: a Baroque gem with glorious views.
** Agrigento: visit the temple complex at sunset.

Opposite: *Isola Bella, Taormina, attached to the coast by a thread of land.*

THE LAND

Sicily is the largest island in the Mediterranean Sea, its size being 25,426km² (9814 square miles). It is triangular in shape with large mountains and hilly tracts divided by **valleys**. The island is on the same latitude as Seville and Almería, in Spain, and the Peloponnese, in Greece. It has a scattering of **islands** to the north (the Aeolian Islands), three small islands to the west (the Egadi Islands) and a long way offshore, nearer to Africa than Italy, there are the islands of Pantelleria, Lampedusa and Linosa.

Mountains

The view, flying towards Catania's airport, is as interesting and colourful as a map of Sicily. Beyond the deep blue of Italy's Tyrrhenian Sea, the narrow shore of the northern coast and the hilly mountains of central Sicily, plumes of smoke identify the island's highest peak,

Mount Etna, which is often shrouded with cloud or smoke. This 3323m (10,900ft) mountain has determined life – as well as death – for many of the island's inhabitants and is visible, on a clear day, from much of the island. It slopes gently down to the fertile Catania Plain and is twinned, on a much smaller scale, by the 986m (3240ft) peaks of the **Iblei Mountains** in the southeastern corner of the island.

Behind the narrow northern shores lies a range of mountains, which is a continuation of mainland Italy's Apennine mountains. They are named, from west to east, the **Peloritani**, **Nebrodi** and **Madonie** mountains. Behind Palermo, and beyond the looming mountains, lies the popular suburban **Conca d'Oro**, which was once a verdant fertile valley. In the far west there are mountains, such as the 1110m (3640ft) **Mount Sparagio**, which rise suddenly from the coast.

Volcanoes

Three of Italy's six active volcanoes are in Sicily and the most threatening is **Mount Etna**, which has been active for over 500,000 years. Its most devastating eruption was in 1669 (*see* page 106) and the eruptions in recent years have also caused considerable damage. Those of **Stromboli** are continuous (and also attract a large number of sightseers) and those of **Vulcano** are periodic. The latter two island volcanoes, located off the northern shore of Sicily, are part of the seven volcanic Aeolian Islands, which also include a handful of submerged volcanic isles. All of these volcanoes are located along the fault which runs the length of Italy, through the Strait of Messina, across and through the Straits of Sicily (where the volcanic islands of **Lampedusa** and **Linosa** are found) and across into the mountains of North Africa.

Those interested in seeing these active volcanoes at closer proximity have a chance to hike up Mount Etna, walk to the peak of Vulcano (with its sulphuric fumaroles), watch the natural fireworks in the night sky around Stromboli, and take radioactive baths along some of Vulcano's shores.

Above: *Never dormant, Mount Etna smoulders and splutters most of the year.* **Opposite:** *The fertile area around Enna in central Sicily.*

Thermal Baths

Due to the lively volcanic activity, Sicily has also been known, since Roman times, for its thermal water. Many springs have been harnessed to form thermal baths (*see* fact panel on page 8).

Rivers and Lagoons

There are few substantial rivers in the country, since the rainfall is not particularly high. Only one natural lake, the small **Lago di Pergusa**, exists. There are, however, underground sources of water and reservoirs, yet in summer these dry to a trickle. The most important river system comprises the four rivers, including the Simeto, which rise in the central mountains and drain eastwards through the Catania Plain. This system provides the fertile plain with

> ### TAKING THE WATERS
>
> Sicily's thermal baths are regarded highly. Perhaps not as sophisticated as those in mainland Italy, they nevertheless have a good reputation. The most popular spots are found in **Selinunte**, **San Calogero**, **Termini Imerese**, **Sciacca** and **Acireale**.

Above: *The beaches around Cefalù are fast becoming popular tourist destinations.*
Opposite: *Vast areas of Sicily are planted with citrus trees.*

excellent irrigation, hence its intensive agriculture. A little further north, the **Alcàntara** has sliced a formidable gorge through the northern slopes of Mount Etna.

Off the western shores is a region of saline lagoons where salt collection is the major industry. These lagoons also provide a haven for sea birds.

Climate

Sicily's climate is one of its charms. It varies, due to the diverse topography and elevation; the coast can swelter with high temperatures, similar to those in North Africa, yet **snow** will fall on Mount Etna in winter. However, since the island is located between latitudes 36.5°N and 38.5°N, it does, generally, have rather **warmer weather** than the northern Mediterranean shores. The average annual temperature is an inviting 18°C (68°F) on the coast and 13°C (55°F) inland.

Northwesterly winds in winter bring some **rainfall** from November to February, especially on the northwestern coast and central highlands, where 1200–1400mm (47–55in) may fall annually, while the eastern shore remains fairly dry with a fall of only 400–600mm (16–24in) annually. In summer, the westerly winds move thunder showers over the highlands, but generally leave the coast dry and subject to hot winds coming from the African continent. Rainfall is expected in late autumn and early spring and although it can rain for days, it can clear suddenly.

Wildlife

If the trend for hunting in the 18th and 19th centuries had not decimated most of the island's wildlife, the land would hold an abundance of both fauna and flora. However, there remain only a few wild mammals (wild cat and wolves are sometimes seen), while the mountainous areas are home to falcons and eagles.

Bird lovers tend to head for the saline areas of western Sicily where the reserves, such as the **Riserva Naturale di Vendicari** and the **Riserva Naturale dello Zingaro**, offer a variety of species.

Snorkellers and scuba divers have the opportunity to experience Italy's best marine life. The **marine reserve** off **Ustica** and the waters around **Pantelleria**, **Lampedusa** (especially known for its marine turtles) and **Linosa** are all renowned. The Aeolian Islands are also abounding in marine flora and fauna.

One of the advantages of Sicily's fertile soil and varied topography is the profusion of plants that flourish, although only 8 per cent of the island is covered with indigenous forest. The natural Mediterranean vegetation comprises **umbrella pines, broom, carob, myrtle, oleanders** and **eucalyptus**. Along the eastern shores, **bougainvillea, oleander** and **poinsettias** all thrive. In the drier areas **cacti** (prickly pear) and **agave** flourish while at cooler altitudes there are **forests** of oak, cork oak and chestnut.

Elsewhere man has planted a variety of palms and cultivated the soil with **olive, pistachio, almond** and **citrus** trees as well as **grape vines** and **caper** shrubs. The slopes of Mount Etna support a wealth of natural and planted species and the blossoms of citrus and cherry are beautiful.

An oddity is the introduction of **papyrus** millennia ago. It grows plentifully along the Ciane River (*see* page 91) and it is said to be the only place in Italy where this Egyptian plant flourishes.

(*see* page 91)

NATURE LOVERS

Apart from **swimming** in the clear waters around the island, visitors can **scuba dive** around the Egadi or Aeolian Islands, at Ustica or off the coast of San Vito lo Capo. **Birders** will find flamingoes in Pantelleria and other waders and water birds in Isole dello Stagnone (near Mozia) and Riserva Naturale dello Zingaro. Birds of prey, such as falcons and eagles, can be spotted in the forest of Ficuzza. **Hikers** can walk to Mount Etna and ramble through the Parco Naturale Regionale delle Madonie. **Cyclists**, too, have the run of the island (the coastal route is fairly flat) and enjoy the southwest coast. Many holidaymakers arrive with their own bicycles. One can also ride **horses** through the Forest of Ficuzza.

KING OF THE SICILIANS

The indigenous Sicilians felt that they were very much second-class citizens under the Greeks. **Ducetius** was a Siculi (see page 109) who proclaimed himself king and led a revolt in 450BC. He gained considerable support and launched an armed attack, against Enna and Akragas, before being overwhelmed by a Syracusan force. Ducetius was allowed to go into exile in Corinth, but secretly returned to Sicily and died in 440BC.

HISTORY IN BRIEF

Sicily's key geographical position ensured the interest of Mediterranean powers. Its history is one of foreign occupation, from Phoenicians to Bourbon monarchs, until it became part of a united Italy in the 19th century. Each invasion has left its mark on the island and contributed to a brilliant cultural legacy, but Sicily's history, since unification, has been one of widespread poverty, emigration and Mafia domination.

Early History

Palaeolithic cave paintings, at least 10,000 years old, have been found on Mount Pellegrino and the island of Levanzo. A new group of settlers arrived on Sicily's east coast and in the Aeolian Islands around 4000BC, leaving incised pottery adorned with patterns, known as *stentinello*. The land was cultivated and trade routes were introduced, which established contact with other Mediterranean cultures. The Sicani, Siculi and Elymni, generally regarded as the island's indigenous population, arrived at around 1500–1000BC. Each group had its own language and culture, and regarded each other with mutual hatred.

Opposite: *A vase unearthed in Naxos, an early Greek colony.*
Below: *The large Bronze Age necropolis, discovered at Pantalica.*

The **Sicani** lived in the west and are thought to have come from either Syria or Libya. The **Siculi**, who lived in the east, came from Liguria (a region of northwest Italy) or Latium (a region of west central Italy). The **Elymni**, in the northwest, claimed descent from the Trojans. According to the Greek historian Thucydides (ca. 460–400BC), the Siculi were responsible for the island's name. After defeating the Sicani in battle, they renamed the island **Sicily** instead of Sicania.

Phoenicians and Greeks

The **Phoenicians**, later known as the **Carthaginians** after their North African colony, established trading bases in the northwest at Motya (today known as Mozia), Panormos (now known as Palermo) and Solunto in the 9th century BC. They were closely followed by the **Greeks**, who drifted to the eastern and southern coasts and founded numerous colonies, including **Naxos** (734BC) and **Siracusa** (Syracuse in 733BC), both of which became **independent city-states**. Most of these settlements were separate from the Sicilian villages, although they began to merge from the 6th century BC onwards and the indigenous population became increasingly **Hellenized**. Corn was a widely cultivated crop and olive trees and vines were also introduced to the island.

The Age of Tyranny

The Greek colonies were ruled by **tyrants**, which at the time simply meant people who seized power instead of inheriting it. With the new settlers, came their native rivalries and the history of Sicily under the Greeks is one of **continual warfare** between cities, although they did form alliances against common enemies, such as the Carthaginians. By the 5th century BC, **Syracuse** was a great city, rivalling Athens in power and prestige. This was effected by the unexpected victory of **Gelon**, the **Tyrant of Syracuse**, against a vastly more powerful and superior Carthaginian force at the **Battle of Himera** in 480BC (*see* panel, page 47).

The golden age of civilization, known as **Magna Graecia** (*see* panel, page 70), brought magnificent **architecture**. The dramatist **Aeschylus** (525–456BC), who is considered the father of Greek tragedy, spent long periods in Sicily. The Syracusan poet, **Theocritus** (ca. 310–250BC), invented the genre of pastoral poetry. **Archimedes** (287–212BC), the great mathematician and physicist, was another notable Syracusan.

LIQUID ASSETS

Archimedes (287–212BC), regarded as the greatest scientist of the Classical world, was born in Siracusa and returned to live there after studying in **Alexandria**. He is best known for the discovery, now named **Archimedes' principle**, he supposedly made while taking a bath. This theory is based on the premise that when a body is partly or wholly immersed in fluid its apparent loss of weight is equal to the weight of the liquid displaced. He is also credited with inventing a device for raising water from the ground (the **Archimedes screw**). Thanks to his ingenious war machines, Siracusa was able to withstand the Romans for three years, but Archimedes was ultimately killed in the siege.

Above: *Roman mosaic in the Villa Casale, Piazza Armerina.*

REVOLTING SLAVES

Under the Romans, Sicily had a vast slave population due to the numerous prisoners-of-war taken in campaigns. Conditions on the *latifundia* were so harsh that in 139BC the slaves revolted. This was led by **Eunus** (as 'king') and **Cleon** (commander-in-chief) and between the two of them they mustered a rebel force of 100,000 men. They took control of Morgantina, Tauromenium (Taormina) and Enna, and held out for seven years until Rome sent in an army. Because of the desperate shortage of slave labour, the **Romans** dealt fairly leniently with the rebels, upon which the empire depended. However, a second revolt in 104BC was brutally crushed and many rebels were shipped off to Rome to fight to the death in the arena.

Under Roman Rule

When the **First Punic War** broke out between Rome and Carthage in 264BC, Sicily became one of the main battlegrounds. This state of affairs resumed in the **Second Punic War** and by this time the Romans were determined to take control of Sicily for good. Greek domination ended in 212BC with the **fall of Syracuse** to the Romans, and by 210BC Rome controlled the whole of Sicily, including the former Carthaginian colonies in the west.

Sicily became Rome's first overseas province. Vast tracts of land were cleared to make way for grain cultivation. Large feudal estates known as *latifundia*, which exist to a certain extent today, were established in the interior and the island became Rome's **breadbasket**. The Greek cities lost most of their autonomy, but the Greek language, calendar and traditions were allowed to prevail. However, veterans who had retired from the army settled on the land and added to the process of Latinization.

Sicily became a popular destination for rich Romans and luxurious **villas** were built, such as the ones found at Eloro, Piazza Armerina (*see* page 77) and Patti. Sicilians became full Roman citizens in AD212 and, at around the same time, **Christianity** began to establish itself on the eastern side of the island.

Barbarians, Byzantines and Moors

In 293 the Roman Empire was divided into the East and the West, and the western half soon became the victim of the barbarian hordes from northern Europe. Sicily was invaded by the **Vandals** during the 5th century. After conquering North Africa, they used Sicily as a stepping stone in order to make their way back to Europe. The Vandals were followed closely by the **Goths**. The Western Empire fell in 476, but the eastern part – centred around Constantinople and renamed

Byzantium – survived. In 535 the Byzantine general **Belisarius** took Sicily for the Eastern Empire, which maintained a tenuous grip on the island for the next three centuries.

The Byzantine conquest established the **Greek Orthodox Church** in Sicily and reaffirmed the Greek orientation of the island. Syracuse was briefly the capital of the Byzantine Empire in the 7th century. However, Byzantine control was soon threatened by **Moorish** (Arab) **raids**, which culminated in a full-scale **invasion** in 827. Palermo was captured in 831, but intermittent warfare continued for the next 70 years until Taormina surrendered in 902.

The Arab conquerors were highly civilized, competent and commercially astute and Sicily prospered, becoming the richest island in the Mediterranean. Some of the vast *latifundia* were subdivided, new irrigation methods were introduced and crops such as cotton, oranges, lemons and sugar cane were planted. During the century of Moorish rule, **Spanish and North African settlers** arrived in their thousands. Art and culture flourished at this time; **Palermo** became a great centre for art and learning.

> ### SARACENS AND MOORS
>
> The Arab conquerors were also known as **Saracens** or **Moors**. Saracen was a term most often used by medieval writers to describe Arabs, particularly those who opposed the Crusaders (namely, the Arabs of Syria and Palestine). Moor first meant an inhabitant of Mauritania, but in the Middle Ages it became a generic term for Muslims from northwest Africa and the conquerors of the Iberian Peninsula. Sicily was subject to raids from both Saracens and Moors, but the invasion force of 827 comprised chiefly Moors. Many Sicilian place names are a reminder of the considerable Arab influence on the island, for example, *calta* (castle) and *gibil* (mountain).

The Norman Conquest

In 1061 the **Christian Crusade** to reclaim Sicily from the Arab infidels began. The Norman Count, **Roger de Hautville** (1031–1101), seized Messina with a handful of followers and gained control of the entire island within 30 years. The new rulers appreciated the Muslims' administrative skills and commercial ability, as well as their culture, and most of them retained their wealth and social prestige.

The Normans were avid **builders** and constructed many castles, palaces and churches in a fusion of Norman and Moorish styles. In 1330 Roger's son

Below: *An example of Arab craftsmanship on a detail from the Palazzo dei Normanni in Palermo.*

THE SICILIAN VESPERS

The revolt known as the
Sicilian Vespers broke out in
Palermo on Easter Monday
1282 at the hour of vespers
(an evening service in some
Christian churches). A French
officer insulted a woman on
the way to church by search-
ing her for concealed
weapons. She fainted in her
husband's arms and he
shouted out, 'Death to the
French!' The officer was
immediately killed and every
Frenchman in Palermo was
massacred. Every other town
in Sicily, except Sperlinga,
followed suit and either massacred or expelled its French
garrison.

(Roger II) was crowned the **King of Sicily**. He was a
ruler of the magnificent, cosmopolitan court at **Palermo**.
Messina also flourished as a port for ships leaving on
crusades. The Normans imported a **baronial class** that
was to have a devastating effect in the centuries to come,
when feudal landowners ruled the land. However, the
liberal regime continued until the death of Tancred, the
natural son of Roger II, sent the succession into the
House of Hohenstaufen and the Holy Roman Emperor
Henry IV made Sicily part of his domain in 1194.

Hohenstaufens and Angevins

Henry IV's son, **Frederick II** (1198–1250), was known as
stupor mundi – wonder of the world. Not only was he a
great scholar and soldier who captured Jerusalem on the
6th Crusade (1229), but he was also a noted patron of the
arts and sciences. Under the Hohenstaufens, Muslims
were discriminated against and transported away in
large numbers. There were **race riots** and, upon the
death of Frederick II, Sicily descended into chaos with
the **over-mighty nobility** filling the void created by the
collapse of the royal authority.

The Pope crowned **Charles of Anjou** the King of
Sicily and Naples in 1265. The Angevin regime was
Draconian (but short-lived) since it was overthrown in
1282 by the revolt known as the **Sicilian Vespers**. The
nobles of Palermo invited **Peter of Aragon** to become
the new king but Charles of Anjou retained his mainland
possessions at Naples, which
also, confusingly, had the
name Sicily.

Below: *A fine legacy
of the decorative Normans,
the landmark red domes
identify Palermo's
San Cataldo.*

Decline under Spain

In 1415 Sicily became an
Aragonese province, ruled
by a viceroy, and in 1442
Alfonso V united Sicily and
Naples, thus creating the
Kingdom of Two Sicilies.
Aragon became part of Spain

and Sicily missed out in the Renaissance developments. The **Inquisition** was imported in 1487 and all the Jewish people were expelled. Intellectual and cultural life stagnated and the country went into a serious economic slump. Money was siphoned off to pay for Spain's religious wars and feudalism still held sway, with the Spanish aristocracy seizing large areas of land. Sicily then declined along with Spain and in 1693 a devastating **earthquake** destroyed most of eastern Sicily.

Above: *The liberator of Italy: Garibaldi strikes a victorious pose in Palermo.*

In the 18th century Sicily passed briefly through the hands of **Savoy** and the Austrian **Hapsburgs** before landing in the lap of the **Spanish Bourbons**, who remained more or less in control until Sicily became part of a united Italy.

Under the Bourbons

During the Napoleonic Wars, Sicily (along with Sardinia) was the only part of Italy unconquered by **Napoleon**. Sicily sided with the British against the French. A large contingent of **British troops** was stationed on the island and the British commander, **Bentinck**, was virtual governor of Sicily. A **constitution** was briefly adopted.

As soon as the British had left, the king repealed all previous reforms and suspended the constitution. Local uprisings were harshly dealt with and rebellion spread across most of Europe in 1848, but when it broke out in Sicily, Ferdinand II became known as *Re Bomba* (King Bomb) for bombarding Messina. Another uprising in Palermo in 1860 inspired **Giuseppe Garibaldi** to choose Sicily as the place to start in his quest to unite Italy.

Unification and Beyond

On 11 May 1860 Garibaldi, a professional soldier who was experienced in guerrilla warfare, landed at **Marsala** with 1000 men who were determined to liberate Italy

17TH-CENTURY HARDSHIPS

The Sicilians had more than their fair share of bad luck during the 17th century. Sporadic outbreaks of **plagues** decimated the population and Mount Etna **erupted** in 1669 with devastating effects. The **earthquake** of 1693 eradicated 5 per cent of the island's population and levelled whole cities.

from foreign domination. With the support of the local
populace, victory was swift and a plebiscite held in
October gave a 99.5 per cent vote in favour of a **union**
with the New Kingdom of Italy under **Victor Emmanuel
II**. Unification did little to change the lot of the vast
majority. Only 1 per cent of the population was eligible
to vote and the opposition was brutally suppressed.
The **Mafia** became increasingly powerful and the **lack
of democracy** and land reform caused Sicilians to
emigrate in droves.

The Twentieth Century

The century began with a catastrophic **earthquake** in
Messina in 1908, which killed more than 80,000 people. In
1922 the fascist leader **Mussolini** marched into Rome and
assumed power. In 1930 his deputy, **Cesare Mori**, was
sent to solve the 'southern problem' and he imprisoned
thousands of suspected mafiosi, which only succeeded in
driving the movement underground. Mussolini took Italy
into **World War II** in 1940 as an ally of Hitler. The island
was heavily bombed and Sicily was the first part of
Europe to be **invaded** by the Allies in 1943.

Postwar Sicily

Sicilians were given control of their own affairs when
regional autonomy was granted in 1946, but the island's
long-standing economic and social problems are still
being resolved. In 1957, Italy became one of the six
founder members of the **European Common Market**
(now the European Union). The economic miracle, subsequently experienced by northern Italy, bypassed most
of Sicily and poverty and Mafia domination are still a
problem. In recent years there has been a concerted effort
by the government to **stamp out organized crime**, which
resulted in a wave of **assassinations** of public officials.

GOVERNMENT AND ECONOMY

Based in Rome, the country's Constitution is formed by a
president, the **Council of Ministers** (or cabinet) headed
by the prime minister, and a parliament comprising a

HISTORICAL CALENDAR

10,000BC Cave dwellers on Mount Pellegrino and the island of Levanzo.
4000BC *Stentinello* culture
15th-10th centuries BC Sicani, Siculi and Elymni arrive.
9th century BC Phoenicians (Carthaginians) establish trading bases.
8th century BC Greek settlers found numerous colonies, including Naxos (734BC) and Siracusa (733BC).
480BC Gelon, Tyrant of Siracusa defeats Carthaginians at battle of Himera.
450BC Ducetius leads native rebellion against Greeks.
212BC Siracusa falls to Rome.
AD212 Sicilians become full Roman citizens.
5th century Sicily invaded by Vandals and Goths.

535 Byzantine conquest by Belisarius.
827 Moorish invasion.
1061 Count Roger de Hautville seizes Messina.
1194 Sicily becomes part of Holy Roman Empire.
1265 Charles of Anjou becomes King of Sicily and Naples.
1282 Sicilian Vespers uprising and Sicily goes to Aragon.
1442 Alfonso V unites Sicily and Naples.
1693 Massive earthquake destroys most of eastern Sicily.
1734 Spanish Bourbons become new rulers.
1806–15 British occupation of Sicily.
1848 Along with most of Europe, Sicily revolts.
1860 Italian unification: Sicily

joins kingdom of Italy.
1908 Earthquake in Messina claims more than 80,000 lives.
1930 Mussolini sends Cesare Mori to solve the 'southern problem'.
1943 Allies invade Sicily
1946 Sicily gains her regional autonomy.
1957 Italy joins the EEC.
1968 Earthquake in north-western Sicily leads to 50,000 people being homeless.
1987 Hundreds of Mafiosi are imprisoned.
1990 Palermo is one of the towns chosen in the Football World Cup Italia.
1992 Two anti-Mafia investigators, Falcone and Borsellino, are murdered.
2001 Mount Etna erupts in a series of violent explosions.

Senate (with 320 members) and a **Chamber of Deputies** (630 elected members). The prime minister heads the Italian government and determines national policy. He or she is chosen by the president and must be approved by parliament. The Senators are chosen from the 20 regions in Italy and serve five-year terms. Since the end of World War II, Italy has had a rapid succession of governments, several cabinet changes and a whole battery of prime ministers. Many of the ministers remain from one cabinet to the next, but this has not been as destabilizing as it seems to be.

Sicily forms one of the country's 20 **regions** called for in the 1948 Constitution and finally

Opposite: *King Vittorio Emanuele II, first king of united Italy.*
Below: *The Italian flag, inspired by the French flag brought to Italy by Napoleon in 1797.*

THE MAFIA

In Sicilian dialect the word *mafia* literally means boldness, which is thought to derive from the Arab word, *mahyah*, for bragging. Following the 9th-century Arab conquest, many Sicilians became bandits in the hills and family loyalties were a priority. Their resistance continued throughout later conquests of Sicily until the 19th century when they had become increasingly powerful and made crime a full-time occupation. The Mafia is still active in Sicilian society today, despite attempts by successive governments to obliterate its power.

set up in the 1970s. Although Rome governs many aspects of life on the island, Sicily does have a fair amount of autonomy. Within this political structure, the region is divided into nine provinces and each of these is subdivided into *comuni* (or municipalities). Headed by a mayor, the *comuni* govern local affairs.

Economy

The island's economy remains largely dependent on its **agriculture**. Orchards (Sicily is Italy's largest citrus producing area) and vineyards provide good returns and wheat, aubergines, peppers, courgettes and artichokes are also cultivated on the island. Its production of **wine**, **almonds** and **olives**, which once provided a substantial income, is now challenged by Spanish produce. Although the Mediterranean suffers from overfishing, the **fishing industry** in Sicily remains important for its catches of tuna and swordfish.

The island's prime industrial area is around Catania where **electrotechnical industries, pharmaceuticals, food** and **engineering companies** are all located. **Petrol** has been found off the coast at Gela and Ragusa resulting in unsightly petrochemical plants in the vicinity of Gela, Augusta and Siracusa. **Minerals** exploited on the island include petrol, potash and small amounts of sulphur although approximately a century ago, Sicily was a world leader in sulphur extraction.

Below: *Petrol reserves and oil refining, near Gela, fill Sicily's coffers.*

There are still some **cottage industries**, though these are becoming fewer, which may be of interest to visitors. They offer a variety of woven rugs in Erice, coral work from Trapani and ceramics from Caltagirone or Santo Stefano di Camastra (there are a number of other towns which are also noted for their ceramics).

Baskets are often produced inland and sold in local markets. Both Petralia Soprana and Ragusa are known for this craft. Ragusa is likewise acknowledged for its exceptional embroidery known as *sfilato ragusano*. It is used for various types of linen and blankets. The tasty, traditional pistachio and almond candies (those fashioned into fruits are known as *pasta reale*) as well as sweets are found in most parts of the island.

Above: *The increasingly liberated youth look toward a brighter future.*

Lastly, **tourism** is an industry that the island would like to develop further. Sicily is already a popular destination for **Italian tourists,** and the package tour industry, catering for sun-starved northern visitors, is also increasing. In addition there have recently been a lot of hotel developments along the coast.

THE PEOPLE

Sicily is one of the most **densely populated** areas in Europe with an average of 190 people per square kilometre around Catania. There is a general migration from the hilly interior to the urban coastal areas where industry offers the hope of jobs and living conditions are perceived to be better.

Sicily is a traditional island – more traditional than mainland Italy – and family values are still upheld, even though the younger generation is increasingly trying to shrug off these principles. In this society, the role of a woman has always been that of homemaker and guardian and today's young women have a hard time breaking out of this mould. In the larger towns, women have a more liberated life, but rural dwellers are in many cases bound by the values of a past era and remain at home with their children.

PUBLIC HOLIDAYS
Capo d'Anno, New Year's Day
Epifania, Epiphany or 12th Night
Lunedì di Pasqua, Easter Monday
Giorno della Liberazione, Liberation Day, 25 April
Primo Maggio/Giorno di Lavoro, Labour Day, 1 May
SS Pietro e Paolo, St Peter and St Paul's Day, 29 June
Ferragosto, Assumption of the Virgin, 15 August
Ognissanti, All Saints Day, 1 November
Immacolata Concezione, Immaculate Conception, 8 December
Natale, Christmas Day, 25 December
Santo Stefano, Boxing Day or St Stephen's, on 26 December

Above: *A traditional wedding in Ragusa Ibla's San Giorgio cathedral.*

Language

Italian is the official language of Sicily, although many locals speak **Sicilian**, which is a dialect. Within the island there are also some seven subdialects which illustrate how little, historically, the different communities intermingled. Interestingly, there is still a small enclave of **Albanian** speakers in Piana degli Albanesi, a part of Palermo province.

Religion

The Sicilians are **Roman Catholics** and religion still plays an important role in island life although, as in other Italian regions, its hold is diminishing. However, there are also places of worship for non-Catholics such as Muslims and Protestants.

Festivals

As with all Latin people, the Sicilians enjoy socializing and celebrating, and their **annual festivals** are colourful affairs which visitors are welcome to attend. Indeed, the Sicilians often appreciate the participation of foreigners.

The **New Year** begins with the usual festivities: **Epiphany** is a public holiday (6 January), which is mainly celebrated by children. The *befana*, an old witch, is supposed to come down the chimney bearing gifts. Agrigento celebrates the flowering of its almonds in the beginning of February, and also in February (or the end of January) is **Carnival** on Mardi Gras (Shrove Tuesday), followed by Ash Wednesday, which marks the start of Lent. The most spectacular carnival is in **Acireale**, but it is also fun at **Sciacca** and **Termini Imerese**.

Easter is particularly important on the Catholic calendar and it is celebrated with mass, processions and re-enactments of Christ's journey to Calvary. It always buzzes with extra markets. If your visit coincides with Easter, make sure you head for **Trapani**, Enna, Erice, Caltanissetta, Prizzi, Marsala or Alcamo to witness this memorable celebration.

GREAT SICILIANS

Archimedes, mathematician, 285–212BC
Antonello da Messina, painter, 1430–79
Alessandro Scarlatti, composer, 1660–1725
Vincenzo Bellini, musician, 1801–35
Giovanni Verga, writer, 1840–1922
Mario Rapisardi, poet, 1844–1912
Luigi Pirandello, playwright, 1867–1936
Giuseppe Tomasi di Lampedusa, writer, 1896–1957
Elio Vittorini, writer, 1908–66

Throughout the rest of the year, local festivals – some religious and some secular – take place. **Patron saints** are fêted on the appropriate day and this usually means a work-free day for the locals. There are fairs and markets and, after the religious ceremonies, processions and general merrymaking take place. If a visit coincides with one of these celebrations, the atmosphere will be superb. Among those to look out for are **Santa Rosalia** in Palermo, **Santa Lucia** in Catania, **San Calogero** in Agrigento, **Madonna della Lettera** in Messina, and **San Giacomo** in Caltagirone.

> **GREAT ARTISTS IN SICILY**
>
> **Francesco Laurana**, sculptor, 1430–1502
> **Caravaggio**, painter, 1573–1610
> **Antonello da Messina**, painter, 1430–79
> **Domenico Gagini**, sculptor, 1430–92
> **Giacomo Serpotta**, sculptor, 1656–1732
> **Antonello Gagini**, sculptor, 1478–1536

Arts and Culture

Thanks to its diverse past, Sicily is one of the most culturally rich islands in the Mediterranean.

Early Remains

Before the Greeks landed in the 8th century BC, the island was already inhabited. Neolithic remains on the Aoelian Islands, now displayed in the **Museo Archeologico** on Lipari, attest to their skills. The Sicani, Siculi and Elymni – whose origins are still vague – also left traces of their civilizations. The keen amateur archaeologist will want to visit tombs near **Lake Desueri** (*see* page 75). These people, who belong to Sicily's prehistoric period, have left their stamp on settlements such as Erice and Morgantina which the Greeks and Romans later appropriated.

The Phoenicians arrived from Carthage (today part of Tunisia) and founded various settlements, three of which – Solunto, Mozia and Lilybaeum (the site of today's Marsala) – are worth exploring. The latter two have museums with fine collections of artefacts.

Below: *2300-year-old amphorae in Lipari's Museo Archeologico.*

FESTIVALS

Carnevale, the week prior to Ash Wednesday, Acireale. The town's famous carnival celebrations.

Sant'Agata, 3–5 February, Catania. Celebrates the patron saint of Catania with processions and fireworks.

Sagra del Mandorlo in Fiore, 1st/2nd week of February, Agrigento. A celebration of the flowering almonds.

Passione e Morte di Cristo, Maundy Thursday, Marsala. Re-enactment of Christ's journey to Calvary and his crucifixion.

Passione e Morte di Cristo, Good Friday, Trapani. An Easter procession and also a procession of hooded penitents.

l'Abballu di li Diavuli, Easter, Prizzi. The Devil's Ball with costumed devils and masks representing the dead in procession.

Santa Rosalia, July 14–15, Palermo. Celebrates patron saint with processions.

Palio dei Normanni, 13 and 14 August, Piazza Armerina. Medieval costumed celebrations and horseback *palio*.

Processione della Vara, 14 and 15 August, Messina. Festivities. 16 August, procession with huge statue in honour of the Virgin.

Santa Lucia, 13 December, Siracusa. Celebrates the patron saint of the town.

Classical Sicily

In eastern Sicily the Ancient Greeks left monuments, which are now in various states of repair. The finest remains are at Naxos, Siracusa, Agrigento, Segesta, Selinunte and Taormina. The Museums in **Agrigento** and **Siracusa** are world class and they trace the development of the respective settlements with exhibits and displays of various utensils, sculptures, architectural decorations and carvings.

The Romans arrived shortly after the Greeks and they wiped out the marauding Carthaginians (as Phoenicians were then known) in the Third Punic War in the middle of the 2nd century BC. They built and rebuilt, employing many of the North African craftsmen from their Empire. A fine example of a Roman villa stands is **Villa Casale**, which is situated just outside Piazza Armerina (*see* page 77). Its mosaics are quite extraordinary. Other Roman remains, built on top of previous settlements, include Eraclea Minoa, Agrigento and Sciacca.

The Norman Legacy

The Norman buildings were of a solid style, but decorated with flair, they also used many of the Arab artisans and produced finely finished buildings. Palermo is filled with good examples of these: **La Zisa** and **La**

Right: *A charming tiled illustration of* Bounty *in Lipari.*

Cuba, the **Martorana** and **Palazzo dei Normanni** with its magnificently decorated **Palatine Chapel**. The cathedral at **Monreale** clearly illustrates the marriage of biblical narrative style from western religion and the decorative styles of the Islamic world.

Gothic Sicily

The troubled years between the 13th and 15th centuries saw many rulers. From this era we have **Castello Ursino** (a castle in Catania) and Catalan-influenced art (in Messina's **Santissima Annunziata dei Catalani**, Siracusa's **Palazzo Bellomo**, and inside the **Palazzo Corvaja** in Taormina). In Palermo, the cathedral's impressive **portico** was also completed in this period.

The Renaissance

It was during the Renaissance years that painting came to the fore in Sicily. **Antonello da Messina** (*see* page 113) was Sicily's greatest Renaissance painter – there are works of his in Messina, Palermo and Cefalù. At the same time there was the emergence of a fine school of sculpture. **Francesco Laurana** spent some years on the island, creating fine portrait busts and delightful Madonnas. The **Gagini** family settled in Sicily and produced some excellent works in Palermo and elsewhere.

Baroque Sicily

Nowhere outside Rome did the Baroque have such a following as in Sicily. It coincided with the aftermath of a notably destructive earthquake and a rise in the island's fortunes. Sicily's rulers and the rich (not forgetting the Jesuits) capitalized on this and brought about magnificent and elaborate churches and palaces with ornate decorative elements. **Noto** and **Ragusa** are Baroque towns and practically every building has a Baroque history. Among the famous architects of this era are **Rosario Gagliardi** (his works are found in Noto, Modica and Ragusa) and **Giovanni Battista Vaccarini** (churches and

Above: *Fabulous decoration around the exterior of the apse of the cathedral at Monreale.*

GIACOMO SERPOTTA, 1656–1732

Sicily's greatest Baroque sculptor, Giacomo Serpotta, was born in **Palermo** where he worked most of his life although he may well have visited **Rome** in his early days as a sculptor. He was a superb master of technique, a keen observer of nature, and possessed a highly developed sense of the decorative. He is particularly noted for his *putti* who frolic joyously amid their religious surrounds. His elder brother, Giuseppe, and his son, Procopio, assisted him.

Above: *A fine Baroque ceiling in a quiet old town, Ragusa Ibla.*

mansions seen in Catania). The luxurious villas surrounding Palermo, and those scattered across Bagheria, merit a visit.

The master of Baroque sculpture was indisputably **Giacomo Serpotta** whose magnificent ornate sculptures grace Palermo's oratories and churches. Sicily produced no great Baroque painter but it did, albeit briefly, offer sanctuary to works of **Caravaggio** (in Messina and Siracusa) and **Anthony Van Dyck** (a canvas in the Oratorio di San Domenico, Palermo).

Liberty Style

In Italy Art Nouveau was known as Liberty and one of its greatest exponents was Ernesto Basile. His son, Giovanni Basile, who designed Palermo's elegant **Teatro Massimo**, followed him. Do not miss Palermo's Villas Malfitano and Florio. Lastly, you can stay in the **Villa Igiea**, another fine Liberty building.

Literature and Music

Sicilian literature started with the philosophical works of Empedocle and Plato, written over 2300 years ago. A love of poetry was later fostered by the Swabian king, Frederick II. The period between the Renaissance and the Baroque also witnessed an increase in literature in Sicily. Classical works were rediscovered on the island and inspired writers such as **Antonio Veneziano** (1543–93). Although most Italian writers expressed themselves in Italian, many Sicilians chose to keep to their native Sicilian dialect.

In the 20th century, Sicily produced two Nobel Laureates: **Salvatore Quasimodo** (the 1959 Laureate) and **Luigi Pirandello** (whose best-known work is *Six Characters in Search of an Author*, published in 1936). Another acclaimed writer was the Prince of Lampedusa, **Giuseppe Tomasi** (1896–1957) who wrote one major work, *Il Gattopardo* (*The Leopard*). It was made into a successful film by Visconti and reached well beyond its geographical borders.

The island was home to two of Italy's famous musicians: **Alessandro Scarlatti** (1660–1725) and **Vincenzo Bellini** (1801–1835). Scarlatti was born in Palermo (though he migrated to Naples) and he wrote over 110 operas and 600 cantatas. His most famous work was *Il Trionfo dell'Onore* (*The Triumph of Honour*). Bellini, born in Catania, wrote the opera *Norma*, his most internationally known work, and the less well-known *I Puritani* and *La Somnambula*.

On the Big Screen

Many movies have been filmed in Sicily, but few have made it big in the anglophone market. Among those to have enjoyed a certain success are *The Postman* (a 1994 production set in Salina) and Luc Besson's 1990 film, *Le Grand Bleu* (The Deep Blue), in which the clear blue seas of the Aeolian Islands play an important role. That classic of the Italian cinema, the 1989 *Cinema Paradiso*, was filmed in an impoverished Palazzo Adriano by the island's most famous cineaste, **Giuseppe Tornatore**, who was born in Palermo in 1956.

Performing Arts

Sicily offers a number of interesting annual events, including arts festivals, which often take place in ancient settings. **Segesta** holds a season of Greek theatre during July and August every odd numbered year, while **Siracusa** has classical performances in its Greek theatre during May and June in the even numbered years.

Taormina's art festival of music, theatre, cinema and dance runs from July to September. **Tindari** opens up its Greek theatre for prose readings during the months of July to September.

At the end of July, **Trapani** stages its Luglio Musicale, a festival of operettas,

---

SICILY IN FILM

Salvatore Giuliano (1961), Francesco Rossi
The Leopard (1963), Luchino Visconti
The Godfather (1972), Francis Coppola
Kaos, Conti Siciliani (1984), Taviani brothers
Cinema Paradiso (1989), Giuseppe Tornatore
Le Grand Bleu (1990), Luc Besson
Giornale Intimo (1993), Nanni Moretti
The Postman (1994), Massimo Troisi

Below: *Homage to one of the island's famous sons, musician Vincenzo Bellini.*

CHINESE PASTA?

The debate is not yet over. Where did pasta originate? Sicilian historians say that this 'Italian' speciality came to Sicily thanks to the Moors who brought it from China. Another theory credits Marco Polo for its introduction from the Orient. Either way, pasta is documented in the island from the 13th century.

classical music and jazz, while **Erice** hosts a programme of medieval and Renaissance music, which is performed in churches. **Catania** also stages a music season from July to September. The major lyrical season is, as elsewhere in Europe, between November and May. At this time **Catania**'s Teatro Bellini, **Palermo**'s Teatro Massimo and **Messina**'s Teatro V Emanuele offer full musical programmes.

Lastly, do not miss the chance to attend a perfor-mance of *pupi* (puppets) while in Sicily. The **L'Opera dei Pupi** (*see* page 42) and the **Teatro di Mimmo Cuticchio**, both in Palermo, stage these puppet plays.

Sport and Recreation

The sport-loving visitor will have a field day in Sicily. Italian speakers should look out for a handy guide, called the *Guida per il turismo alternativo*, which lists ideas for the visitor and the sport enthusiast. **Skiers** can take to Mount Etna's north-facing slopes, near Linguaglossa, between December and February.

Hikers may ascend Mount Etna, either alone (seek professional advice first) or in small groups, from Rifugio Sapienza. **Nature lovers** and **birders** should head for the Riserva dello Zingaro (*see* panel on page 58), Parco delle Madonie or Parco dei Nebrodi. **Cyclists** should bring their own bikes, although they can be rented through the Federazione Ciclista Italiana (tel: 091 6718711) in Palermo. The coastal routes offer fine views and fairly untaxing itineraries.

Water sport enthusiasts will find that most resorts rent out the basic gear for **canoeing** and **windsurfing**, while small dinghies and catama-rans can likewise be hired. **Scuba divers** should head for the offshore islands to be sure of clear waters and a wealth of marine flora or fauna. Tiny **Ustica** (with its marine reserve), the **Aeolian Islands** of Panarea and Salina, and the far more dis-tant islands of **Pantelleria**, **Lampedusa** and **Linosa** are all renowned for their submarine environment.

Left: *The Vendicari Reserve is a popular place among cyclists.*
Opposite: *A large Sicilian puppet fashioned in the form of Orlando.*

SICILIAN ICE CREAM

It was the Arabs who introduced this popular treat to the Sicilians. They created the frozen confection, using **snow** from Mount Etna and the **lemons** from the mountain's slopes, for which Italy, and in particular Sicily, has become famous.

Food and Drink

Simple yet varied, Sicilian fare owes its diversity to the many civilizations, which – at one time or another – colonized the island. Plato, Pliny and Horace all refer to it in their writings, and subsequently even more ingredients have been introduced. It was the **Arabs** who lifted Sicilian cuisine from mere sustenance to sensational, with the introduction of rice, citrus fruit, pasta and cane sugar. The **Spanish** brought potatoes, tomatoes and peppers, while the **French Bourbons** introduced *la cuisine française* and spread the influence of Neapolitan dishes.

Italian meals consist of a number of courses: the *antipasto*, an *hors d'œuvre*; *primo piatto*, a starter; *secondo piatto*, the main dish; *contorno*, the vegetable dish; and the *dolce*, the dessert. *Formaggio* (cheese) is usually taken before, or instead of, the dessert. Sicily is rich in local produce (capers, olives and their oils, pine and pistachio nuts, almonds, fresh *ricotta* cheese, sun-dried salt and subtropical fruits) and the cuisine is usually enjoyed with one of their many local wines (*see* page 29).

Antipasto is a wonderfully tempting array of cold dishes, which includes salamis, marinated fish, seafood, vegetables and cheese. It is usually at a buffet table and charged either by plate, selection or weight. *Primo piatto* is either a pasta or rice-based dish. **Pasta** favourites

CLASSICAL SICILY

There are some 25 major archaeological sites in Sicily dating from preclassical days and surviving both the Greek and Roman occupations. Remains from these include a number of theatres, which are still in use (during the summer season) for performances of both classical and modern drama. The most important venues are **Taormina**, **Segesta**, **Siracusa** and **Tindari**. Details of performances can be obtained from the AAPIT offices of the provinces in which these theatres are situated, or on the website from the AAPIT in Palermo: www.aapit.pa.it

Above: *Imaginatively sculpted marzipan fruit on sale in a confectioners.*
Opposite: *Florio has a fine marsala winery and retail shop open to visitors.*

include *pasta alla Norma* (made with aubergine, tomato, onion and dried ricotta cheese), *pasta con le sarde* (with sardines, anchovies and fennel), pasta with all kinds of seafood, and those well-loved pastas such as lasagne, cannelloni and ravioli. There is little that can compete with the home-made dishes. *Gnocchi*, a distant pasta cousin, are made with ricotta cheese, but shaped into cocoons and served with a variety of sauces. *Gnocchi di patate*, made from potato, are also delicious.

Rice is an important *primo piatto*. **Risotto**, a variety of moist, flavoured rice dishes, will include saffron, vegetables, mushrooms, cream, seafood or, in the case of *risotto nero*, squid and its black ink. Rice is also the basis of that popular snack, *arancini* (little oranges). Flavoured not with fruit, but with ham or tasty meat sauces, these fried rice balls are delicious.

During the cooler winter months, thick soups are *de rigueur*. *Minestra* (soup) can be made with a variety of vegetables – we've all come across *minestrone* with its white kidney beans and potpourri of garden veggies.

Carne (meat) is traditionally well-seasoned goat or **lamb**, but there is also veal in the form of *involtini* (parcels of veal stuffed with dried fruits and almonds) – the Sicilians love these Arab-inspired recipes – and *Vitello alla Marsala*, slices of veal cooked in Marsala wine (or *Pollo alla Marsala*, if substituted with chicken).

Pesce (fish) is on all the coastal menus, but it is expensive. Look out for *tonno* (tuna), *pesce spada* (swordfish), needlefish, sardines, *acchiughe* (anchovies), *calamari* (squid) and *arragosto* (lobster). Apart from grilled or baked fish, one should try the delicious *Cuscusu alla Trapanese*, a soupy fish couscous, and *Involtini di spada*, which are parcels stuffed with swordfish. Fish meets vegetables with *finocchio alle sarde*, fennel with sardines, which can also be combined to make a delicious pasta (*see* page 28).

Vegetables are usually ordered separately and, apart from myriad salads, these include courgettes, beans, aubergines, broccoli and spinach. They are sometimes served cool and seasoned with olive oil and lemon juice.

Desserts to look out for include the island's famous *gelati* (ice creams) and *granite* (iced sorbets), its creamy *cassatas*, such as the now famous *cassata granita frutta di Martorana* (with dried fruits and marzipan), and the tube-like *cannoli*, which is filled with a smooth and sweet sheep's milk ricotta.

Sicily's **cheeses** are usually made from sheep or goats' milk. Ricotta, pecorino, provolone and cacciocavalli are among the most popular.

Pizzas are also found all over Sicily and the most classical are the Napolitana and Margherita pizza. The *fruatte* is a homespun anchovy and onion pizza.

> ### MARSALA, SICILY'S PREMIER WINE
>
> The rich, sweet taste of marsala (akin to the taste of port) seduced the palates of many a northern European during the 19th century. It was **John Woodhouse** (the first English entrepreneur to taste and appreciate the wine), **Ben Ingham** and his nephew **Joseph Whitaker** who did much to improve and promote the wine. **Vincenzo Florio** and **Pellegrino** (better known as a bottler of mineral water) also entered the market and today they are the largest marsala producers in Marsala. It is a DOC wine (from a specific area) and improves with the further addition of alcohol during the process.

Sicilian Wines

Sicily produces 20 different wines, 17 with a DOC label (meaning top class – *see* page 96); some stand up to international competition and the rest provide good table wines. Look out for the white Alcamo and Capo Boeo. Good red wines include Etna Rosso, Donnafugata, Regaleali and Cerasuolo di Vittoria. Slightly stronger dessert or apéritif wines include Malvasia di Lipari, marsala (*see* panel, this page), Moscato di Pantelleria and Zibibbo.

2
Palermo Province

Once the most cosmopolitan city after Constantinople, Palermo has a rich and extended history. It is a city blessed with a warm and dry climate, and it stands on the northern shores of the island, facing the Tyrrhenian Sea.

Established by the **Phoenicians** in the 7th century BC, Palermo prospered under the Arabs in the 9th century AD and again later under the **Normans**. During the rule of kings Roger II and Frederick II, it attracted intellectuals and artists from far and wide. It was a period of construction, not to be matched until the **Baroque** days of the 17th century. In the 1800s Palermo developed its trade links, including the export of Sicilian wines, to Great Britain. A legacy of this era are the numerous luxurious villas in the city suburbs as well as those that dot the countryside around Palermo.

Due to internal strife, racketeering and competing trade links, Palermo has sadly degenerated since those heady days. Today its appeal rests with its past, though its spirit is alive and now fighting back. Some restoration has rejuvenated its tired buildings and more is expected.

The city is divided into areas, all of which can be explored on foot, though local buses make journeys to the more distant monuments easier and quicker. The maze-like Arab quarter, the impressive Norman heart, grandiose Baroque monuments and the orderly **Liberty** area of town merit a few full days of exploration.

Further afield, the city of **Monreale**, the Baroque villas at **Bagheria**, the medieval resort town of **Cefalù** and the mountains of the **Madonie** are all of great value.

Mare Tirreno (Tyrrhenian Sea)
I. di Ustica
Isola Eolie
Palermo
Cefalù
Isola Egadi
Mare Ionio (Ionian Sea)
I. di Pantelleria
Mare Mediterraneo (Mediterranian Sea)

DON'T MISS

*** **Palazzo dei Normanni:** in Palermo, with its mosaics.
*** **La Cattedrale:** massive, beautiful and historical.
*** **Monreale:** cathedral with fabulous mosaics.
** **La Martorana:** in Palermo, for more mosaics.
** **Serpotta's stucco:** decorations in Palermo's oratories
** **Cefalù:** monuments and beaches.
** *Pupi* **theatre:** for a performance of string puppets.
* **Catacombs:** preserved, aristocratic mummies.
* **Palermo's markets:** busy and vibrant.

Opposite: *The landmark cupolas of San Giovanni degli Eremiti.*

QUATTRO CANTI AREA

Palermo's two most important streets – Via Vittorio Emanuele and Via Maqueda – meet in **Piazza Vigliena** (better known as Quattro Canti or Four Corners). The piazza, which is now rather soiled by vehicle pollution, was originally named after the 17th-century Spanish Viceroy, the Duke of Vigliena. It is the city's focal point, not just because of the two thoroughfares that pass through it, but also because of its beautiful 17th-century palaces and elaborate fountains nearby. The palaces, redolent with Baroque ornamentation, shimmer in their wealth of classical decoration. Doric, Ionic and Corinthian orders decorate their façades.

Piazza Pretoria ***

Just a couple of minutes along Via Maqueda lies Piazza Pretoria with, as its centrepiece, the spectacular **16th-century fountain** designed by Florentine Francesco Camilliani for a Tuscan commission. However, Camilliani died and his son sold the work to the Senate of Palermo. It has little in common with most Italian fountains, as it is huge, decorated with four flights of steps, embellished by numerous sculptures and crowned with a central fountain. The naked sculptures caused a considerable stir when they were first unveiled and the work was known as the 'shameful fountain' for quite a number of years.

Palermo's stately town hall, the mustard-coloured Renaissance **Palazzo delle Aquile** (named for the eagles which decorate its façade, but also known as the Palazzo Municipalità Palermo), is open to visitors when not in formal use. On the other side of the square, the west wall and dome of the pinkish church of **Santa Caterina** dominate the piazza, although its entrance is on the smaller Piazza Bellini (named for the Teatro Bellini which used to be here) just behind it.

The flanks of **San Giuseppe dei Teatini** (open in the mornings and late afternoons), which is on the far side of Via Maqueda, belie the richness of this church's lavish Baroque interior. Take time to admire the detail in the stucco work, the columns and the statues in the vault.

La Martorana **

Dominating Piazza Bellini is the 12th-century bell tower of **La Martorana**, which somewhat overshadows the church itself. This solid Norman church (open in the morning and from 15:30 to dusk) is named after Eloisa Martorana who, in 1143, founded a Benedictine convent (once next door).

> **FROM CHURCH TO POST OFFICE**
>
> Separated from La Martorana by distinguished palm trees, the Norman **San Cataldo** was built in the 12th century. It has merlons and blind arches on its outer walls and three red cupolas (its trademark) cap it. It seems far more Arab than Norman, and the church's intimate interior is remarkably plain by comparison. It was even used as a post office at one stage.

Opposite: *Narrow, noisy and sometimes seedy, but always interesting – the backstreets of Palermo.*
Below: *The interior of La Martorana, one of the finest surviving buildings of the medieval city.*

SHOPPER'S DELIGHT

The most important transversals off Corso V Emanuele are **Via Marqueda** and **Via Roma**, the old town's most fashionable area for shopping. Saturdays and certain annual 'car-free' days turn these, and neighbouring streets, into a pleasant pedestrian-only zone. This is something to be thankful for in this traffic-filled city. The shops extend from Quattro Canti, through **Piazza Verdi**, along the **Via Ruggero VII** and into the Art Liberty part of the town, **Via della Libertà**.

The church was built for the convent slightly later, possibly with the assistance of artisans from Constantinople. Some of the original Norman structure still exists, including the beautiful mosaics, though much has been modified over the centuries. The soaring vaults are patterned with rich colours and myriad decorations. Columns, saints and cherubs all represent the different epochs of ecclesiastical decoration.

Returning to Via Maqueda and travelling south (if you were to turn to the north, you'd be heading towards the Liberty or Art Nouveau part of town), you will reach the 18th-century **Palazzo Comitini**, which was constructed for the Prince of Gravina and is actually an amalgam of two palaces. The highlight of this palazzo is the **Sala Martorana** with its fine woodwork, Murano crystal chandeliers and Rococo mirrors.

Corso Vittorio Emanuele ✱✱

Also known as del Cassaro, this is one of the city's main thoroughfares. It runs from the port right up to what was the royal palace. It was the link between the political, religious and municipal powers. Today it is busy and often congested, but it is still characterized by elegant buildings.

La Cattedrale ✱✱✱

A garden of palms leads the visitor to the city's large and striking cathedral. Much has been altered and enlarged over the centuries (it was first a Christian basilica, became a mosque under the Muslims, and was reconsecrated by the Normans). Palermo's cathedral dates from the 12th

Below: *The striking exterior of Palermo's cathedral.*

century. Parts of it are quite beautiful and others marry the subsequent styles less successfully. The southern **portico** is a good example of Catalan Gothic architecture – note the intarsia work, the sculpture and even the inclusion of a Koranic script. The lacy decoration and geometric designs of the exterior also hark back to the building's Muslim days (open until 19:00 and closed during lunch in the summer months).

The most interesting features of the interior are the chapels with their **royal sarcophagi**. Here the mortal remains of **Sicily's early kings** are encased in dark porphyry. Amongst the nobles lies Roger II, the island's first king; his daughter Constance and her husband, Henry IV; Federico II and his wife, Constance of Aragon (in a dark red sarcophagus of Roman origin), and various other Aragonese royalty.

Above: *The seat of the Regional Assembly, Palazzo Normanni.*

Palazzo dei Normanni ***

It is likely that the first building to be erected on this site, now occupied by the Norman Palace (open Monday, Friday and Saturday mornings), dates back to the Carthaginians. Documents written during the Saracen era make mention of the building and although the emir moved to the Kalsa district of Palermo, this area was again in vogue when the Normans took possession of Sicily. Later the Spanish added the façade. Part of the palace is used today as the seat of Sicily's parliament (the **Assemblea Regionale Siciliana**).

The highlight of this unusual building is its **Cappella Palatina**, the Palatine chapel (open every morning and from Monday to Friday in the afternoons), built by Roger II in the mid-12th century. This glorious building melds the finest Arab-Norman decorative elements and also borrows from antiquity. The 10 classical columns supporting the arches between the three naves, and the scintillating mosaics above, are surely one of the greatest European achievements of this era. The Lebanese cedar ceiling, floating in the best of Arab traditions like a cavern of delicate stalactites, is a marvel. The Pascal candle, too, is decorated with rich motifs.

On the second floor, the **Sale del Re Ruggiero** (King Roger) is also a 12th-century masterpiece with its mosaics depicting bucolic hunting scenes. Note the fine

Above: *The gardens and cloisters of San Giovanni degli Eremiti, Palermo.*
Opposite: *The solid façade of the Palazzo della Zisa, built under the Normans.*

details in the animals, the flora and the delicate decorative elements along the lower walls.

As you leave the Palazzo dei Normanni, stroll in the beautiful gardens of **Villa Bonanno** next door.

San Giovanni degli Eremiti ★★★

It was Roger II who also commissioned the building of San Giovanni degli Eremiti (open every morning and from Monday to Friday in the late afternoons) in 1132. Its five sienna-coloured domes are visible from the gardens and confirm the King's choice of Arab architects. With their semitropical blooms, the **gardens** are also a charm. It is a pleasant place in which to contemplate the small chapel, its cloisters with their thin, twin-columned arches (once part of a monastery) and the remains of the small mosque. Like many public buildings, the little complex bulges with tourists on Sundays.

Chiesa del Gesù ★★

The **Jesuits** arrived in Sicily in the mid-16th century and, bringing considerable Spanish funds with them, they built their first church (open in the morning) behind Via Marqueda on Via Ponticello. The elaborate work of the Chiesa del Gesù's interior is in flagrant contrast to the very run-down residential neighbourhood, the **Albergheria**, around it. This beautifully decorated Baroque church suffered damage in World War II, but has been well restored so that the intarsia and sculpture are again as they were intended. Look up at the vibrant ceiling frescoes depicting the life of **Philip Neri** who was an important figure in the **Italian Counter Reformation**. Admire the sculpture, particularly the 18th-century work, on the inside of the façade. In some parts of the nave, the sculptural decorations are so three-dimensional they seem to be practically freestanding. Sculptor Serpotta was again responsible for many of these.

Chiesa del Carmine *

Not far from the church of the Gesù, the superb majolica-tiled dome of the Chiesa del Carmine presides over the colourful stalls of the **Mercato di Ballarò**. This market, situated in the poor neighbourhood of the Quartiere dell'Albergheria, dates back to Saracen times.

Palazzo della Zisa *

This ancient palace to the west of the town centre is accessible by bus or taxi. The honey-coloured Palazzo della Zisa (open every morning and from Monday to Saturday in the late afternoons) is another fine Norman building, constructed under William I in 1164, in what was then the hunting grounds for the Norman kings (now one of the less picturesque of Palermo's suburbs).

This solid, rectilinear palace has had a chequered history. From **hunting abode** to **fortress**, it passed into disrepair until it was restored in the late 1900s. Many elements, such as the hanging, vaulted ceilings (with the stalactite effect), the loggias around water, the fountains and the golden mosaics, recall the finest of Arab architecture. On the first floor, a small collection of artefacts, including 11th-to 13th-century ceramics and fine Egyptian wooden screens, are on display.

Another Norman example is the palace not far from the Palazzo dei Normanni, **Palazzo La Cuba** (corso Calatafimi 100), which was built in 1180 by William II. Despite restoration, there is not a lot to see, but a model on display gives a good idea of how it sought to emulate La Zisa.

> ### CATACOMBI DEI CAPPUCCINI
>
> For a totally different experience, take a trip to the Capuchin Catacombs (Via dei Cappuccini, open each morning and afternoon). It is interesting, if a little macabre: **8000 aristocratic mummies** await inspection, in an unusually good state of preservation, while one, in particular, of a little girl who died over 80 years ago, is in such a fine state that you'd think she'd just fallen asleep. The mortal remains of Sicily's most famous author, **Giuseppe Tomasi di Lampedusa** (who died in 1957), rest in the Capuchin cemetery nearby.

LIBERTY STYLE

Sicily's interpretation of the Art Nouveau movement, prevalent in Britain and Belgium in the 1890s, was known as **Stile Liberty** (the Liberty style). It was named after the famous London department store, which championed Art Nouveau designs. The basis of this decorative and architectural style was nature and its forms (such as plant tendrils) and it was transposed into decorative or architectural details and used for wrought-iron work, glass windows and furniture. There are some fine Liberty-style buildings in **Palermo** and **Messina**.

Opposite: *Palermo once produced some of the most exquisite horsecarts.*
Below: *Renovated, the Teatro Massimo is a Liberty-style gem.*

NORTHERN PALERMO

This area is the more modern part of Palermo and it is an elegant district where most of the construction and avenues date from the early 19th century. Wandering through, you'll see imposing buildings decorated with detailed wrought-iron motifs and impressive balconies which all bear evidence of the floral **Liberty style** (*see* page 24). This is the area in which wealthy Palermo citizens choose to live, if indeed they remain within the city limits – the part of Palermo where the Smart Set prefer to shop and dine.

Teatro Massimo ★★

Guiseppe Verdi gave his name to the piazza in which this theatre is situated, and the theatre was inaugurated with a Verdi opera when it opened in 1897. Built in a neoclassical style by Giovanni Battista Basile and finished after his death by his son, Ernesto, it was one of Europe's three largest opera houses (seating 3200 spectators), but it was closed for 20 years in the late 1900s. Thanks to recent renovations, this beautiful theatre has been reopened for use. Outside there are two interesting kiosks that were designed by Ernesto Basile and epitomize the grace and beauty of Art Nouveau. The website for ticket sales of shows and opera performances is www.teatromassimo.it

Villa Malfitano ★★

Supposedly inspired by a Florentine villa, the Villa Malfitano on Via Dante (open in the morning from Monday to Saturday) was built by an Englishman, Joseph Whitaker, in 1887. It basks in a beautiful 7ha (17-acre) garden, which has some interesting and rare trees. Joseph was the talented nephew of Ingham

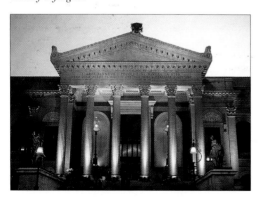

Whitaker, one of the great exporters of Italian marsala wine, and made a name for himself not only with ornithology and botany, but as an amateur archaeologist who excavated much of the island of Mozia (*see* page 60). The villa was modified and embellished over the years to become a good example of the Liberty style. It enjoyed much

success with the English expatriates and the visiting European royalty including George V of England.

Museo Archeologico Regionale ★

Housed in what was formerly the 16th-century Convent of Olivella, this museum (open in the mornings) has a diverse wealth of prehistoric and Roman archaeological remains. Look out for the 2500-year-old sculpted metopes, from the frieze of a temple at Selinunte, recounting Ancient Greek myths. The Greek, Roman and Carthaginian bronzes (in particular the Hellenistic ram from Siracusa) are also fascinating. There are plenty of Greek ceramics (like most of the items, they are not particularly well labelled) including some with delicate black figures and others with red. There are also some interesting mosaics dating from early Roman times.

Galleria d'Arte Moderna ★

Located in the neoclassical Teatro Politeama (just next to the Air Terminal) is another Liberty-style building, the Modern Art Gallery (open in the mornings from Tuesday to Sunday). It has a good collection of 19th- and 20th-century Italian art, sculptures and canvases, including works by local Sicilian painters. Amongst the latter is a self-portrait by **Renato Guttoso** (1912–87), the political and social realist painter. There are also works by **Italian Futurists**, Carlo Carrà (1881–1966) and Gino Severini (1883–1966).

SICILY'S COLOURED WAGONS

Sicily's brilliantly coloured and beautifully painted traditional **horse-drawn carts** are practically extinct. Allusions to these are the small doll-sized replicas found in souvenir shops, but the real item is a magnificent work of art that began to make its appearance in the middle of the **19th century.** The wagons were used as vehicles of work for the (better-off) country folk. The tradition was strong in Palermo and Catania. Each centimetre of wooden surface – wheels, base, side walls and struts – were **carved** or **painted** predominantly in red with details of yellow, blue and green. The panels were traditionally decorated with scenes from **heroic battles**. Even the horse's tackle was decorated with **embroidery** and, on its head and mid-back, two-coloured, **feathered details** were attached in the form of a spouting fountain.

Above: *Ballarò market is Palermo's prime address for food products.*

PALERMO'S MARKETS

Palermo has a number of interesting street markets which should not be missed. They open in the mornings and close in the early evening. For food produce, there is little to match the labyrinthine **Ballarò** market, which sprawls through the Albergheria district between the Gesù and San Nicolò churches. **Capo**, just off Via Carini and in the district of the same name, is another busy produce market that also sells clothes. **Vucciria**, in the Vucciria district near the port, is known for its fish market and was beautifully portrayed in a painting by Guttoso. The **Papireto Flea Market** (selling bric-a-brac, furniture, prints and lamps) is located on Piazza Peranni, just beyond the cathedral, in Via Bonello.

LA CALA TO LA KALSA

The area located directly behind the old port is known as La Cala. Its history reflects the **Saracen** and later the **Christian** dominance in Palermo. Through the mêlée of streets and past some imposing palaces, you'll find your way into La Kalsa, (the area taking its name from the Arab word for pure, *halisah*). It's a poor part of town but one which is very interesting, and the architecture has a distinct oriental flavour recalling the days when the Arab emirs and their ministers favoured this section of Palermo.

San Domenico ★★

The elegant Baroque façade of San Domenico (Piazza Domenico, open every morning and late on Saturday and Sunday afternoons) with its columns, niches for sculpture and statue of its patron saint, St Dominic, sets the tone for Palermo's favourite church.

The highlight of San Domenico is, however, the **Oratorio del Rosario di San Domenico** in the building beside the church. The interior is a joyous hymn to Baroque decoration by **Giacomo Serpotta**. Stucco elements unfurl and release angels and putti. The main altarpiece is by **Van Dyck** (1599–1641) and it shows the Virgin of the Rosary with St Dominic and the patronesses of Palermo. It was painted in the early 1620s and is not a typical work by this Dutchman

More extraordinary decorative work by the Baroque master of stucco, Giacomo Serpotta, can be seen in the **Oratorio del Rosario di Santa Cita** (enter via the Chiesa Santa Cita) just a few minutes away. You will be rewarded by the sight of beautiful rows of angels and virtues seated on elaborate architraves. Note that cloister visits are by appointment only.

San Francesco d'Assisi *

This church (open each morning and late afternoon, except on Sundays) dominates the pleasant Piazza San Francesco d'Assisi. It was founded in the 13th century, but it has been damaged, remodelled and restored to such an extent that little remains of the original building. It is, nevertheless, an impressive structure and its interior is spatially harmonious. Look at the **rose window** on the façade above the original and attractive portal.

The nearby **Palazzo Mirto** (open each morning and afternoon, but mornings only on Sundays) was the residence of the **Lanza Filangeri** family who, from the start of the 17th century, occupied the palace for over 250 years. Of particular interest are the 18th-century stables where each stall is decorated with the bronze head of a horse.

A few minutes' walk from the Palazzo Mirto is the **Piazza Marina** and the **Giardino Garibaldi** (not to be confused with the delightful Giardino Inglese, off Via Libertà). The garden, brimming with fig and ancient banyan trees, is surrounded by fine period palaces such as the **Palazzo Chiaramonte**, which dates back to the beginning of the 14th century. It was then home to the Spanish Viceroys and served in the 17th and 18th centuries as the tribunal for the Inquisition.

Museo Internazionale delle Marionette **

The elaborate and large *pupi*, as puppets are known in Italy, played an important role in Sicilian drama. The island's puppet theatres are famous and this museum, at via Butera 1 (open every morning and late afternoon, from Monday to Friday,

> **SNACKING IN SAN FRANCESCO**
>
> Just opposite the church of San Francesco is one of the town's oldest eateries: the **Antica Focacceria San Francesco**. Renowned for its *focaccia* (flat bread made with olive oil), this 19th-century snack bar serves up hot sandwiches using tasty morsels of veal, spleen, heart or, if you are not a carnivore, ricotta cheese. It is worth a visit for its historical interior (even if you are not tempted by the **focaccia**).

Below: *Well-maintained Giardino Inglese, in the Liberty part of Palermo.*

Below: *Sicilian puppet
shows rank highly in the
world of marionettes.*

and on Saturday mornings), groups puppets from Sicily
and Naples (the other great Italian centre of puppetry)
with marionettes, hand puppets and shadow puppets
from many other parts of the world (in particular, Asia,
where the tradition is still very much alive in rural
areas). The museum is a must for children. There is even
a small puppet theatre on the premises and a studio
where children can make their own puppets.

Galleria Regionale della Sicilia **

In the Palazzo Abatellis, via Allora 4 (open every morning and on Tuesday, Thursday and Friday afternoons), is
the **Regional Gallery of Sicily**, which holds a collection
of predominantly medieval Sicilian sculptures and paintings. The high-ceiling palace was built in the last decade
of the 15th century for Francesco Abatellis, who was
appointed by the Spanish as master pilot, and manages
to combine Catalan Gothic with Renaissance architectural elements. The exhibits have been very well
displayed and it is a joy to explore this museum.
Highlights include the enormous fresco *Triumph of
Death* (originally in the Palazzo Sclafani), the delicate
marble bust of *Eleonora of Aragon* by Francesco
Laurana, the *Portrait of a Young Man* by Antonello
Gagini (who also produced various sweet-faced madonnas), the painting of the *Annunciation* by Sicilian
Antonello da Messina (1430–79), Saracenic ceramics
and Arabic architectural
details, including some
magnificent door jambs.

Orto Botanico **

The Saracens brought the
custom of well-laid-out,
and often scented, gardens
to Europe and particularly
Sicily. The **Orto Botanico**
botanical garden (open
in the mornings from
Monday to Saturday), next

to the 1777 Villa Giulia, was laid out in 1789 and is a fine example of such a garden. A diverse wealth of subtropical species flourish in the clement conditions of Palermo and many of the more unusual plants, usually found elsewhere, can be identified amongst the fine specimens here. The *Ficus magnolioides* (the huge **flowering fig tree**), exotic bamboo and the original lily pond can all be found here.

Taking the route back towards central Palermo, you'll pass the renovated convent of **Santa Maria di Spasimo** (the road shares the name).

Near Santa Maria di Spasimo are the remains of the Norman church, **La Trinità** (more popularly called La Magione), founded in 1197. It was severely damaged during World War II, as was the piazza in front of it. However, both have been partly restored and the church is worth a visit for the unusual doorways which characterize its façade. In Piazza Magione a small memorial plaque is dedicated to **Giovanni Falcone**, the Sicilian magistrate who was assassinated while presiding over a Mafia trial in 1992.

Above: *A Byzantine Madonna from the Galleria Regionale della Sicilia.*

SANTA MARIA DI SPASIMO

This church and its convent, founded in the beginning of the 16th century, have had a chequered history and over the last few centuries they were used as a hospital. In the 1980s, a comprehensive renovation programme was initiated and the building (minus its roof) was finally given back to the community, to be used as a cultural centre for exhibitions as well as concerts.

AROUND PALERMO

The area around Palermo is rich in monuments. Most sights can be visited in a morning or at most during a day's excursion.

Monreale ★★★

The most important place to visit, only 8km (5 miles) southwest of Palermo, is Monreale. It dominates the green flanks of the **Conca d'Oro** (the Valley of Gold) and was once a tranquil rural area, but it is now flecked with an ever-increasing number of private homes and apartment blocks. This town is renowned for its well-

preserved Norman Benedictine abbey, founded in 1174 by William II. The highlight of this notable complex of buildings is the Duomo – or cathedral – (open each morning and late afternoon) with its fabulous **mosaics** and fine **cloisters** (it is open each morning and in the late afternoons from Monday to Saturday and mornings only on Sundays and public holidays).

The solid 12th-century bronze doors open into the Duomo, constructed around an 18-columned nave. The unique simplicity of the Duomo serves to heighten the magnificence of its scintillating coloured mosaics, said to cover a surface of over 6300m^2 (64,000 square feet), which represent some of the finest religious craftsmanship in Europe. **These 12th- and 13th-century mosaics**, depicting biblical scenes, embellish the entire apse and the upper walls with the visual rendition of both the Old and New Testaments. Presiding over the entire illustration is a figure of **Christ**, hands raised in blessing. William II, the founder, is also depicted on two mosaics in the choir. The delicate architectural decoration of the exterior of the apse – similar to that of Palermo Cathedral – is also worth looking at.

The **cloisters** adjoining the Duomo are no less spectacular. They are an **architectural masterpiece** and an intricate feat of delicacy and beauty. Myriad different designs characterize the pencil-thin **twin columns** – some carved and others inlaid with coloured marble – and their different carved capitals are inspired by both

A FINE VIEWPOINT

On Caputo Hill, opposite Monreale, lies the **Castellaccio**. This building was originally designed as a convalescent home for Benedictine monks in the 12th century. It was subsequently fortified and then suffered both destruction and rebuilding. It is located just off the road (a footpath zigzags up through the pine trees from the road to the remains) to San Martino delle Scale. The impressive **panoramic views** of Monreale are most spectacular in the late afternoon.

Christian and medieval themes. Supported by the columns and capitals are elegant, pointed Gothic arches. Climb onto the Duomo's roof for overviews of the cloisters and the sweeping **panorama** of the town.

Solunto **

One of Sicily's three important Punic sites, Solunto (open every Monday to Saturday and mornings only on Sundays and public holidays) has a marvellous position overlooking the Tyrrhenian Sea. The **Carthaginians** founded the city in the 4th century BC and it enjoyed considerable prosperity for some 500 years.

To get an overall perspective of this rectilinear town, study the plans in the museum (through which you pass to enter the excavations) and then head off to visit the principal sights. These include the remains of the **Terme**, the public baths, and the house where a mosaic was found depicting Leda and the swan (via the main street of **Via dell'Agora**). The route then takes you to the brick-paved **Agora**, the public assembly or meeting place, and behind this are the remains of a small Odeon (perhaps used for concerts). Nearby are the fairly indistinct remains of the semicircular theatre.

On higher ground, to the north of Palermo and situated between Mount Pellegrino and Mount Castellaccio, there are many villas, which were constructed during the 18th and 19th centuries. These homes afford the well-to-do residents with cooling breezes and fine views towards Palermo.

> **FINGERS OF SEA**
>
> If you are visiting Solunto, don't miss the coast towards **Capo Zafferano**. Take a drive down to **Sant'Elia**. It is an extraordinary coastal village where the sea extends like long fingers into the landmass. The picturesque **San Nicilicchio** conversely occupies the 'fingernail' of another of those promontories. The third attractive settlement is **Porticello**.

Opposite: *The cloisters of Monreale's cathedral are Norman masterpieces.*
Below: *The important Punic archaeological site at Solunto.*

Mount Pellegrino *

The imposing peak of Mount Pellegrino (much praised by Goethe for its beauty) rises to 605m (2000ft) and from the summit there is a superb **panorama** of both northern and eastern Sicily. On the mountainside there

BAGHERIA

Just 16km (10 miles) east of Palermo lies Bagheria, which is known for its collection of fine **Baroque villas**. There are approximately 16 superb 'country residences' belonging to former Palermo-dwelling nobles. The two most impressive are **Villa Palagonia** (open to the public in the mornings), with its quirky grotesques, and **Villa Butera**.

MADONIE'S OLD VILLAGES

There are a number of old, traditional villages within the Park of Madonie which offer a glimpse of rural Sicilian life. Many have a colourful folklore and interesting customs. Visit one of the following: Polizzi Generosa, Cerda, Gangi, Geraci Siculo, Petralia Sottana and Petralia Soprana.

Below: *The shores of Sicily provide ample opportunity for large- and small-scale fishing.*

is a popular sanctuary, **Sanctuario di Santa Rosalia** (open in the mornings and afternoons), and a 17th-century chapel hewn from the rock and dedicated to Santa Rosalia who is thought to have died here. When her mortal remains were brought down to the plague-ridden town, the epidemic stopped and she was thus declared patron saint of Palermo.

Mondello *

Located approximately 11km (7 miles) north of Palermo, Mondello is one of the city's favourite beach areas with a sandy shore extending approximately 2km (just over a mile) in length. Fashionable **villas** have been built here over the past two centuries and the beach still enjoys a certain prestige, although it is largely divided into beach clubs with bathing huts and beach chairs. It does not have the cleanest of Sicilian waters, but it offers a respite from the summer heat.

FURTHER AFIELD FROM PALERMO

Some 55km (35 miles) northwest from Palermo lies the solitary island of Ustica. Alternatively the northern coast leads one to the ancient town of Cefalù and further into the Madonie Mountains.

Ustica **

Part of a submerged volcano, this small island is home to some 1350 inhabitants and extends a mere 8.6km² (5 square miles). It has, however, a large transient population of visitors attracted to the island's simple lifestyle and the well-run **marine reserve**, which offers a fine opportunity for snorkelling and scuba diving. There were inhabitants on this island as early as the 3rd century BC (the

archaeological museum has exhibits from this era) and probably as far back as the Bronze Age. Today's locals are mainly fishermen, although they are increasingly becoming involved in tourism.

The island's pretty little settlement is centred around its port, **Cala Santa Maria**. On the west coast, between Cala Sidoti and Caletta, the **Riserva Naturale Marina** (which is divided into three zones – each with different degrees of ecological protection) offers interesting opportunities to explore the marine world. Ustica's isolated position has ensured a varied marine flora and fauna, some of which can be enjoyed by snorkellers. Various guided scuba tours are also available. For those who do not want to wet their feet, the **aquarium** recreates a number of different marine environments, complete with flora and fauna.

The drive along Sicily's north coast, and through the eastern reaches of Palermo province, hugs the coast and is accompanied by the railway line. The road passes through **Termini Imerese**, an industrial port which owes its origins (albeit over 2300 years ago) to the thermal waters surging from the ground at 43°C (110°F), around which various baths were constructed. These are still running at the **Grande Hotel delle Terme**.

Above: *Cefalù is an appealing combination of ancient town and attractive beaches.*

HIMERA

Some 18km (11 miles) east of Termini Imerese lie the Greek ruins of Himera (open daily). The settlement was founded in 648BC, as a colony of Zancle (today's Messina), in a strategic position providing access to the heart of the island. It was the scene of the crushing defeat of the Carthaginians in 480BC when they were attacked by the combined Greek troops from Agrigento and Siracusa. However, they wrought vengeance just 72 years later and wiped out the city. What remains of those belligerent times is the **Tempio della Vittoria** (a building in the Doric order).

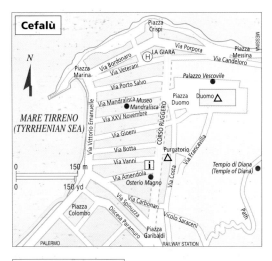

Cefalù

N

MARE TIRRENO
(TYRRHENIAN SEA)

0   150 m

0   150 yd

PALERMO

Piazza Crispi
Via Porpora
LA GIARA
Piazza Messina
Via Candeloro
Via Bordonaro
Via Veterani
Piazza Marina
Palazzo Vescovile
Via Porto Salvo
Via Mandralisca — Museo Mandralisca
Piazza Duomo
Duomo △
CORSO RUGGERO
Via XXV Novembre
Via Gioeni
Via Botta
Purgatorio △
Via Vanni
Via Francavilla
Tempio di Diana
(Temple of Diana)
Via Amendola
Osterio Magno
Via Costa
Via Carbonari
Via Spinuzza
Discesa Paramuro
Vicolo Saraceni
Path
Piazza Colombo
Piazza Garibaldi
RAILWAY STATION
MESSINA
Via Vittorio Emanuele

Cefalù **

The most eastern town in Palermo province, Cefalù, is a very picturesque fishing port wedged between the ocean and a rocky promontory. The town is divided in two parts by the pedestrian-only Corso Ruggero, an artery which separates the narrow streets of the medieval western Cefalù from the modern and orderly street plan of the eastern part.

Rising above this small town is its **Duomo** (open every morning and late afternoon), a Norman cathedral begun by Roger II in 1331. Artisans from the **Byzantine** and **Arab** world were responsible for much of the cathedral's decoration. Beautiful **capitals** crown the columns lining the nave and a number of **Norman beams** cover the ceiling. The central apse boasts some excellent original **mosaics**, though it is not certain whether they were executed by the Greeks or the local artists (under the instruction of Greek artisans).

The large oeuvre of coins, books and art works, collected by Baron Enrico di Mandralisca, was bequeathed to the town on his death and now constitutes the eclectic **Museo Mandralisca** (Via Mandralisca, open every morning and afternoon). The most notable work is a small but fine portrait of an unknown man by the Messina born **Antonello da Messina**, one of Italy's greatest artists. Other items include **majolica**, an ornithological collection and well-presented archaeological remains from Lipari. Do not miss the street-side glass window facing the palace cellars where the large terracotta pots, formerly used for storing olive oil, are displayed.

Cefalù has become increasingly popular in recent years and many resort hotels have opened along the beaches attracting tourists from northern Italy and beyond. King Roger II had the Duomo built to give thanks for the refuge of Cefalù's beaches, after he was involved in a storm.

Parco delle Madonie **

Part of the Madonie Mountains, which rise behind Cefalù, has been gazetted as a protected reserve.

Not often visited by other European tourists, the 40,000ha (160-square-mile) Parco delle Madonie fans out from its highest peak **Pizzo Carbonara** – at 1979m (6590ft) – and forms an area of varied terrain which supports plants found in northern Europe, northern Africa, western Asia and the Mediterranean. Porous karst rock has led to a series of underground tunnels and reservoirs and in some parts of the reserve the landscape is noticably devoid of surface water which, elsewhere, resurfaces in torrents and falls.

Hunting has decimated much of the larger mammal population, although recently there have been efforts to reintroduce once-indigenous species to the region. Interestingly, **falcons** are now bred in Geraci Siculo. You could be lucky enough to sight wolves, weasel, wild cat and martens, as well as peregrine falcons and eagles overhead. Alternatively, animal lovers can hire horses and trek through the beautiful countryside, which features cork, pine and oak forests.

Take time to explore the medieval towns of **Pollina** and **Castelbuono**; both are easily accessible. Pollina boasts an unusual theatre and Castelbuono has, among its many historic buildings, a forbidding castle housing the **Cappella Palatina**: a chapel that has fine stucco work executed by Serpotta.

PALE GREEN GOLD

Olives have a long history and they are common in Sicilian cuisine. They have been used commercially for over 2000 years and through the last couple of decades they have enjoyed a distinction (the '**Mediterranean diet**' of fish, fruit, vegetables and olive oil has become synonymous with healthy living) not previously seen. Their output has increased considerably and some 95 per cent of world production centres on the Mediterranean countries, with Italy being one of the main suppliers of olive oil. Sicily's oil is rich and sometimes heavy. The various categories of oil are **extra virgin** (the finest), which has less than 1 per cent acidity, **virgin**, having between 1 and 2 per cent acidity, and olive oil (without the word 'virgin'), which has below 3.3 per cent acidity.

Below: *The Duomo dominates the heart of ancient Cefalù.*

Palermo Province

BEST TIMES TO VISIT

The climate is mild. **Winter** is rarely severe although it is the rainy season. **Autumn** and **spring** are very pleasant with occasional showers, and the **summers** are hot and dry. However there are always places to beat the heat. Palermo celebrates its patron saint, Santa Rosalia, with processions on 14 and 15 July.

GETTING THERE

Palermo has one of the island's two international airports, which is located 30km (19 miles) out of town at Punta Raisa. Palermo's **Falcone Borsellino Airport** (tel: 091 6019111 for domestic flights and tel: 091 591275 for international flights) is easily reachable. Taxis and regular buses (tel: 091 580457, Autolinea Prestia and Comandè, for details) link the airport to Palermo. Bus services from the airport also go directly to other Sicilian towns. For information contact AST (tel: 091 6882783 or 091 6882906) or SAIS Autolinee (tel: 091 6166028). The second international airport in Sicily is located just outside Catania, (**Fontanarossa Airport** tel: 095 349837/1654). There are bus services which link Catania with Palermo (2hr and 40min) and other towns. A **railway** line runs through Palermo and some trains travel directly to and from Rome

or Naples. For information tel: 1478 88088 (toll free) or Website: www.fs-on-line.com Palermo can also be reached from mainland Italy by sea. One may **sail** between Palermo and Naples (11hr), Livorno (17hr) and Genoa (20hr). Contact Grimaldi Grandi Navi Veloci, tel: 091 587404, or Tirrenia Navigazione on their toll-free line, tel: 1478 99000.

GETTING AROUND

It is best to **walk** within the town, though you can take taxis or buses. There are eight major **taxi** ranks in town as well as radio taxis (tel: 091 512727/513311 or 091 225455/225460). Palermo City buses (AMAT) are often crowded. Try to use the minibus circular buses, **Linea Giallo** or **Linea Rosso**, which pass through the narrower streets and include many important tourist sites. Regular **bus services** link Palermo to all the major cities of Sicily. Catania takes just 2hr 40min on the motorway. Information for SAIS buses on Via Balsamo, tel: 091 6166028, and for AST buses on Piazza Marina, tel: 091 6882783/2906. **Train** travel from Palermo is slow, but convenient for short trips.

WHERE TO STAY

LUXURY
Central Palace, corso V Emanuele 327, Palermo,

tel: 091 336666, fax: 091 334881, e-mail: cphotel@tin.it Renovated palace hotel in centre of old Palermo.
Villa Igiea Grand Hotel, salita Belmonte 43, Acquasanta, Palermo, tel: 091 543744, fax: 091 547654, e-mail: villa-igiea@tin.it Beyond city on beachfront.
Grotta Azzurra, Località San Ferlicchio, Ustica, tel: 091 8449048, fax: 091 8449396, e-mail: grottazzurra@ framon-hotels.com Mid-sized luxury hotel on this tranquil island.

MID-RANGE
Excelsior Palace, via Marchese Ugo 3, Palermo, tel: 091 6256176, fax: 091 342139. Old-style palace in the centre of Liberty area.
Hotel Europa, via Agrigento 3, Palermo, tel/fax: 091 6256323. In Liberty Palermo. A modern hotel with simple, comfortable rooms.
Baglio Conca d'Oro, via Aquino 19c/d, Borga Malora, tel: 091 6406286, fax: 091 6408742. Small hotel in refurbished 18th-century winery.
Splendid Hotel La Torre, piano Gallo 11, Mondello, tel: 091 450222, fax: 091 450033, e-mail: latorre@latorre.com Renovated hotel near beach with good views.
Residence Torre Artale, contrada Sant'Onofrio 1, Trabia, tel: 091 8100111, fax: 091 8100777, e-mail:

Palermo Province

info@torrerartale.com
once an aristocratic home,
with private beach.
Kalura, via V Cavallaro 13,
Località Caldura, near Cefalù,
tel: 0921 421354, fax: 0921
423122. Beach-side hotel

BUDGET
Hotel Sausele, via Vicenzo
Errante 12, Palermo, tel: 091
6161308, fax: 091 6167525.
Close to station. Inexpensive,
well run, clean and central.
Hotel Letizia, via Bottani
30, Palermo, tel/fax:
091 589110, e-mail:
hotelletizia@neomadia.it
In the midst of Kalsa.
Hotel Corona, via Roma 118,
Palermo, tel/fax: 091
6162340. Modernized, very
central and inexpensive.
La Giara, via Veterani 40,
Cefalù, tel: 0921 421562,
fax: 0921 422518. Small hotel,
close to coast and centre.

WHERE TO EAT

LUXURY
Charleston, piazza Ungheria
30, Palermo, tel: 091 321366.
Closed Sundays. A popular
restaurant for the well heeled.
Santandrea, piazza
Sant'Andrea 4, Palermo,
tel: 091 334999. Traditional
regional cuisine. Booking
necessary. Closed on Sundays.

MID-RANGE
Lo Scalino del Cardinale, via
Bottai 18, Palermo, tel: 091
331124. Excellent Sicilian specialities. Open for dinner only.

Cambio Cavalli, via G
Patania 54, Palermo, tel: 091
331560. Piazza Olivelli area.
Difficult to find, but worth the
effort. Closed Mondays.
Trattoria Lo Bianco, via Eico
Amari 104, Palermo, tel: 091
585816. Long-standing
favourite, closed on Sundays.
Ristorante La Brace, via XXV
Novembre 10, Cefalù,
tel: 0921 423570. Excellent
value and imaginative cuisine.

BUDGET
Chez Mazzara, corner of Via
Magliocco and Via Vaglica,
Palermo, tel: 091 321443.
Best ice creams and sorbets.
Le Volte, via Agrigento 12,
Palermo, tel: 091 6259999.
Excellent pizzas and inexpen-
sive Palermo specialities.
Casa del Brodo, corso V
Emanuele 175, Palermo,
tel: 091 321655. Good, fami-
ly-run restaurant, inexpensive.
Kandisky Café, via Libertà
12, Palermo, tel: 091 329100.
Street-side café for the smart
set in Palermo.

SHOPPING
Palermo has a wide range of
shops. The area along, and

between, Via Roma and Via
Marqueda is the prime
shopping zone while the big
names in fashion are found in
Via della Libertà.

USEFUL CONTACTS
Ufficio di Turismo, piazza
Castelnuovo 35, Palermo,
tel: 091 6058111/5827881
or, for a reduced tariff,
tel: 167 234169,
Website: www.aapit.pa.it
Ufficio di Turismo, corso
Ruggero 77, Cefalù,
tel: 0921 421050.
Ufficio di Turismo, salita
Belmonte 1, Villa Igiea,
Palermo, tel: 091 540122 (for
information on Monreale).
Main Post Office, via Roma
322, Palermo.
Siremar, via Crispi 120,
Palermo, tel: 091 336631.
British Consul, via Cavour
117, Palermo,
tel: 091 326412.
American Consul, via
Vaccarino, Palermo,
tel: 091 305857.
Alitalia, via Mazzini 59,
Palermo, tel: 091 6019111.
Sicilia nel Terzo Millenio,
Palermo. Useful information,
e-mail: rdinoit@yahoo.it

PALERMO	J	F	M	A	M	J	J	A	S	O	N	D
AVERAGE TEMP. °F	55	55	57	60	66	73	79	80	76	70	62	58
AVERAGE TEMP. °C	13	13	14	16	19	23	26	27	24	21	17	14
HOURS OF SUN DAILY	4	5	6	7	8	10	10	9	8	6	6	4
RAINFALL in	2.8	1.7	2	1.9	0.8	0.4	0.1	0.7	1.6	3	2.8	2.4
RAINFALL mm	71	43	50	49	19	9	2	18	41	77	71	62
DAYS OF RAINFALL	15	15	15	12	8	4	2	3	7	12	16	16

3
Western Sicily

Remote, yet within easy reach of Palermo and Agrigento, the western extreme of Sicily is one of the most interesting areas. The coast of this triangular island extends into the Mediterranean Sea and stretches out towards Tunisia on the tip of the African continent. It has much in common with Africa and indeed many of the inhabitants are of African origin and were lured to the island, in the past, by its economical success and a climate similar to that of Africa.

The capital of this western most province, Trapani, is a pleasant fishing port with some unexpected, interesting buildings in its historic pedestrian centre. Within sight of the town lie the offshore Egadi Islands and to the north, beyond the lovely hilltop town of Erice, lies the beautiful **San Vito lo Capo**, which is a popular beach resort area.

The high-speed *autostrada*, between Palermo and Trapani, skirts around the ancient settlement of **Segesta** (one of the island's most important and stunningly situated classical sites). A second important site is the coastal town of **Selinunte** on the way to Agrigento. There is the warm coast south of Trapani, known for its **salt pans**, the unusual island of **Mozia**, and the town of Marsala, which gave its name to the island's most famous dessert wine, **marsala**. It is an area of distinct African ambience and one with an interesting and rich bird life. Not to be missed, either, is the town of **Mazara dell Vallo**, a lively fishing port with a small but fine historic heritage.

DON'T MISS

*** Erice: town on top of a hill with stunning views.
*** Segesta: magnificent setting for a perfect temple.
** Trapani: known for its salt and coral.
** San Vito lo Capo: beautiful, sandy beaches in a spectacular setting.
** Marsala: wine tasting in a historical town.
* Riserva Naturale dello Zingaro: one of the region's fine nature reserves.
* Selinunte: visit the overgrown remains of a 2500-year-old city.

Opposite: *Windmills are used to pump sea water for Trapani's salt production.*

TRAPANI

Facing out towards the west, the town of Trapani lies within close proximity to the Egadi Islands. Its history dates back to Roman times, when it was known as **Drepanon**. Most of what one sees today dates from the 16th century or later. Interestingly, **Edward I** received news of his accession to the English throne here (returning from the Crusades in 1272). The town suffered a degree of damage from the air raids during World War II.

Trapani is a medium-sized town of some 70,000 inhabitants and it owes its prosperity to its former reputation for **coral** and the salt pans in the marshes. After a period of neglect, these have been reactivated to provide a lucrative industry. The **Salt Museum** just to the south of the town is also worth a visit.

Centro Storico ★★

The old part of town, on the tongue of land lapped by the sea, has a fine historic atmosphere. The medieval area, in the western part of the town, hides some attractive period buildings amidst its narrow streets. The 16th-century **Palazzo Ciambra** (also known as Palazzo della Giudecca), in the old Jewish quarter, was built in a highly decorative Plateresque style (note its embossed towers). Just beyond it lie the lovely tropical gardens of **Villa Margherita** – a focal point in Trapani. A short walk down the corso brings you to **Santa Maria del Gesù**, a 16th-century church with a Catalan portal. The interior boasts an enamel terracotta of a *Madonna and Child* by the Florentine sculptor Andrea della Robbia (1435–1525).

A couple of blocks from the tourist information office is the **Chiesa del Collegio dei Gesuiti**: a Baroque building with a façade incorporating caryatids and putti. A block away, and alongside the elegant **Corso Vittorio Emanuele**, lies the town's Baroque **Cattedrale di San Lorenzo**. Its construction began in 1635 to replace an earlier 13th-century church. Although its portico is rather abrupt, the interior of the cathedral is light and airy and it is crowned, as are a number of churches in Sicily, with a dome of dazzling green tiles.

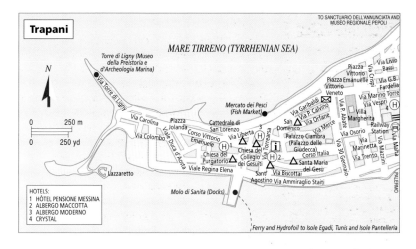

MARE TIRRENO (TYRRHENIAN SEA)

Trapani

HOTELS:
1 HÔTEL PENSIONE MESSINA
2 ALBERGO MACCOTTA
3 ALBERGO MODERNO
4 CRYSTAL

Between **Piazza Vittorio Veneto** (the modern heart of the town) and the Torre di Ligny runs **Via Garibaldi**. Torre di Ligny was formerly a 17th-century fortress erected by the Spanish and is now the **Museo della Preistoria e d'Archeologia Marina** (open each morning and afternoon). Via Garibaldi is a street with plenty of fine, renovated palaces and churches. Although the palaces are not open to the public, locals talk with respect about their superlative *saloni*. Just to the north is the **Mercato dei Pesci** (the town's morning fish market).

Sanctuario dell'Annunciata ★★

In the eastern part of Trapani, on Via Pepoli, lies the 13th-century Sanctuario dell'Annunciata (open in the mornings and late afternoons), built by the **Carmelites**. The original **rose window** above its Gothic portals is particularly fine, but most of the structure dates from its rebuilding in the 18th century. The **Cappella dei Pescatori**, built in 1481, is a pretty chapel dedicated to the wellbeing of local fishermen and it has a beautiful, small, frescoed cupola. **Nino Pisano** (1315–68), the son of Florentine Andrea Pisano, is said to be the author of the delicately crafted *Madonna and Child* – one of Sicily's most beautiful Gothic sculptures – in the

Opposite: *The sanctuary of the Madonna of Trapani.*

Above: *Pretty Carmelite cloisters, now part of the Museo Pepoli.*

JEWELLERY FROM THE SEA

Coral has, for centuries, been one of the mainstays of Trapani craftsmen. Coral (a colony of living organisms found in warm waters at a depth of between 10 to 20m) reefs grow around the **western islands** of Sicily and the **Pelagian Islands** (Lampedusa). This craft originated in the 15th century when local craftsmen carved **rosary beads** from coral. As their skills matured, they sculpted religious objects, picture frames, lamps, jewellery and cribs.

A very fine collection of coral can be viewed at the **Museo Pepoli**, and shops in **Trapani** and **Taormina** sell coral (and imitation-coral) jewellery.

Capella della Madonna. The Baroque **belfry** rises above Trapani's suburbs, a landmark in this somewhat flat town.

Museo Regionale Pepoli ★

This regional museum (Via Pepoli, open every morning and afternoons only on Tuesday) is located in part of the 15th-century Carmelite complex. It is reached through the elegant cloisters and has a collection which dates from prehistory to the 19th century. The ground floor is dedicated to sculpture and the first floor has displays of **Neapolitan** paintings (a *Pietà* by 14th-century artist Roberto di Oderisio and works by the 15th-century Pastura) and decorative arts. Look out for the painting of *The Stigmata of St Francis*, which was painted in 1530 and attributed to **Titian**.

Among the well-exhibited items on display on this floor are the intricate pieces of 17th-century **sculpted coral** (one of Trapani's specialities) and a collection of decorative items fashioned by local silversmiths, sculptors and jewellers. There are also a number of small figurines destined for **nativity crèches** – another speciality of southern Italy – including fine pieces by Giovanni Matera. The same sculptor also produced the 16-frame *Massacre of the Innocents*, which is on display elsewhere in the museum. Before leaving, stop a while to admire the impressive staircase which leads from the ground to the first floor.

Erice ★★

One of the most beautifully situated towns in Sicily, Erice boasts a tiny population of 350. But what **views** these inhabitants enjoy! Erice is perched at 750m (2500ft) on the summit of a rocky outcrop, with an endless expanse of deep blue sea is at its feet. The town has experienced periods of much greater population and notoriety. During **Phoenician** times there was an active cult involving the **goddess of fertility** which the Greeks and Romans continued, changing only the goddess's name. Sited high on the headland, the statue became synonymous with the protection of mariners. The much-treasured altar was destroyed in 260BC.

The charm of this unusual and quaint little town lies in its intimate atmosphere. Narrow paved streets, blind walls and sturdy doors hide tiny patios and small courtyards. In summer it is bathed in sunlight and in winter it can be enveloped in mist and cloud – lending it a romantic and mysterious air.

The views are stunning as you climb up to Porta Trapani to enter this small town. Erice is, as you'll soon realize, laid out in the form of an equilateral triangle, but the tiny streets make following directions far from easy. As you enter the **Porta Trapani**, the fortified **Chiesa Matrice** on the left (open mornings and mid-afternoons) is the first monument of note. Its Gothic exterior (the rose window is a later addition) is superior and its unusually decorated ceiling is also of exacting workmanship. In the usual tradition, some of the building stone was pilfered from the earlier **Temple of Venus** located just beyond both the **Giardino del Balio** and what remains of the 12th-century Castello.

Wandering away from the main thoroughfare, Via Vittorio Emanuele, you'll happen upon the **Centro Ettore Majorana** and the impressive **town walls**, the latter dating as far back as the Carthaginians, both on the western side. You will also see a number of churches including **Santa Orsola** (Addorlata), near the Norman **Porta Spada** at the northern extreme of town, **San Carlo**, and the deconsecrated **San Domenico** on the attractive piazza of the same name. Do not miss the wax nativity scenes and the various other exhibits in the **Biblioteca Comunale** (free entrance and open each morning and afternoon).

You'll notice beautifully coloured woven rugs in many of the shops in this area and this is one of the specialized crafts for which Trapani is particularly noted.

Below: *A 19th-century reconstruction of a Norman castle, owned by the Pepoli family.*

CAPE SAN VITO

Sheltered between Capo San
Vito and Capo Roma and just
some 40km (25 miles) north
of Trapani, is the large Golfo
di Castellammare. Part of this
pristine area has been desig-
nated a natural park, the
**Riserva Naturale dello
Zingaro** (open daily from
sunrise to sunset), which is a
fine reserve with six lovely
beaches and a wealth of bird
life. The whitewashed village
of **San Vito lo Capo**, dominated by the sheer cliff face
of the Cape of San Vito, has
developed into a delightful
resort with good beaches
and translucent, clear waters.
It clusters around its 18th-
century church, which had
Saracen origins.

Egadi Islands **

Offshore from Trapani lie the three Egadi Islands of
Favignana, **Levanzo** and **Marettimo**. Their remote location and beautiful coasts – 15–30km (10–19 miles) from
Trapani – lure nature lovers, scuba diving enthusiasts
and marine archaeologists. For this reason they have
been declared a **marine reserve**, in order to protect their
flora and fauna. In 241BC the islands witnessed
Catullus's historic victory for Rome over the powers of
Carthage, which signalled the end of the First Punic War.
Remains show that the islands were indeed inhabited in
prehistoric times and archaeological artefacts recovered
suggest that the islands were on a busy shipping route.

The largely flat islands used to survive on fishing and
the cutting of tufa for building stone. Today tourism
does much to fill the coffers. This area of Sicily was
noted for its tuna, and the island of **Favignana** had a
large fishery that (under the entrepreneurial Florio family who owned the islands from 1874 to just before
World War II) had an excellent reputation. The annual
mattanza, a tradition of catching and killing huge shoals
of tuna, takes place over a few days, between mid-May
and mid-June, around Levanzo and Favignana.

The island of **Levanzo** is small and sparse in vegetation and, with just a handful of inhabitants, it is strictly
for lovers of remote places. It is littered with caves, and
the one that made this island world famous is **Grotto del
Genovese**, where 33 drawings of prehistoric man were
discovered in 1949. The slightly larger **Marettimo** is
more promising. It, too, is wild, but its simplicity and
beautiful landscapes prove
to be very attractive to
some **nature lovers**.

Just over 110km (69
miles) from Sicily's shore,
the island of **Pantelleria** is
yet a further destination
for those seeking wild,
remote and unspoiled
islands. Living in simple,

Below: *On clear days
their are stunning views
from Erice towards Capo
San Vito.*

white, cube-like houses that owe more to Africa than Europe, the locals produce their own sweet **muscatel wine** and fine **capers**. The island is unusual in having both African and semi-Alpine vegetation within such a small area.

Segesta ★★★

The Ancients chose their sites well. On the sloping flanks of Mount Barbero, between Trapani and Palermo, Segesta is the perfect location for a theatre and a temple (open daily from morning until one hour before sunset) and it is a must on any traveller's journey. Many of the buildings still remain to be discovered, but the well-preserved temple is reason enough to make the trip.

Above: *Segesta's beautifully intact temple dates from Greek times.*

Like Erice, Segesta probably owes its origins to the **Elymians** and it soon became an important city in the **Hellenes**, indeed rivalling Selinunte in the 4th century BC. Destroyed by the Siracusan Agathocles in 307BC, the city was reborn under the **Romans**, occupied by the **Normans** and then abandoned in **medieval** times.

The **Doric temple** is one of antiquity's best-preserved temples and its solitary position serves to underline its architectural harmony and perfection. Erected in 430BC and carved from honey-coloured limestone, all 38 smooth columns, both the pediments and the entablatures are intact. Since it has no cellar, archaeologists puzzle whether it was unfinished or built for a cult.

The **theatre** is some 2km (just over a mile) up the hillside and it is accessible either by shuttle bus or by foot . (this is not for the faint-hearted, but it does give one the time to admire the panoramic views and enjoy the wild flowers and birdsong). The theatre was built in the 3rd century BC and it is a perfect hemisphere hewn from the hillside. It measures some 63m (70yd) in diameter, and it faces the azure blue waters of the Golfo di Castellammare. Biennial **theatre performances** of ancient plays are offered in this spectacular setting.

SURVIVING THE RUINS

Sicily's many archaeological sites take their toll. Many are large and, in summer, extremely **crowded** and **hot,** so a bit of preparation is a good idea. Take comfortable, **closed shoes** without heels. The ground is rough and there are sometimes snakes (a notice at Eraclea Minoa will draw your attention to this). If there is a **bus service** to reach more distant points (such as at Segesta), rather pay and take it. Wear a hat and **sunglasses** and, in summer, take **sunscreen** and a **shirt**. A **bottle of water** is essential.

Above: *The Norman church of San Nicolò Regale, Mazara del Vallo.*

THE COASTAL ROUTE

To the south of Trapani, low, square houses decorate the hot and dusty panorama and all is reminiscent of Africa. This land is perfect **salt mining** territory. The combination of heat and evaporation ensure that the saline waters soon shed their moisture and leave behind crystals of salt. **Windmills**, heaps of dirty salt protected by stacked tiles and the rectangular pans all remain as testament to a national industry that was once far more esteemed, controlling much of the European salt trade. Other man-made features of the landscape are the *baglie* (fortified buildings previously used as wine distilleries and cellars). In between, along the saline shores, wild duck and herons are abundant.

Mozia **

The small island of Mozia was once an important Phoenician colony, founded in the 8th century BC. It stands in saline lagoons and both Siracusans and Carthaginians coveted this strategic position. The **Siracusans** won the territory in a fierce battle. The island was the property of **Joseph Whitaker** (*see* page 38), **marsala** exporter and amateur archaeologist, who was responsible for starting excavations on the island. The Whitaker villa is now a local museum and it displays simple **Phoenician ceramics**, Greek vases (with both red and black figures), statuettes, sculptural remains and the fine marble sculpture of a tunic-clad young man (dating from the 5th century BC). The ruins include a **necropolis**, **Punic walls**, the so-called **Casa delle Anfore**, named for the amphorae unearthed there, and the artificial lake, **Cothon**, whose purpose is still puzzling archaeologists. The island is now owned by the Whitaker Foundation and only a few families live here.

THE FLORIO FAMILY

Brothers, **Paolo** and **Ignazio Florio**, were born in the 1770s in Bagnara Calabra, but moved to Palermo as youths. They opened up a drugstore and became famous for their various remedies and health drinks. As the family business flourished, they expanded into wines, ceramics, a foundry and a steamboat company. They bought the **Egadi Islands** in 1874 and were pillars of Palermo society, hosting such notables as Kaiser William II, Ferdinand of Austria and Kings George V and Edward VII. The company sadly declined after the war and its various interests were sold off.

Marsala **

The hot Sicilian summers produce a strong, sweet wine, marsala, which takes its name from this elegant town. It was named by the Muslims who called it *Marsa Allah*, meaning the port of Allah. Known for centuries, the wine is still produced here and exported worldwide. A visit to one of the main **marsala producers** – such as Florio or Pellegrino (purveyors of marsala and water) – is well recommended. Marsala's roots go back to the Carthaginians who erected this town (once called Lilybaeum) in the beginning of the 4th century BC. Numerous Tunisians live here and it has a distinctive African feel to it. Marsala is busy throughout the year and is particularly well known for its **Maundy Thursday** religious procession.

The **Cattedrale**, located on Piazza della Repubblica in the middle of the old town, was established in Norman days and extensively restored in the 18th century. Among the most valuable items inside it are the 15th-century statues by members of the **Gagini** family, notably Antonino, Giacomo and Domenico. Nearby, the **Museo degli Arazzi Fiamminghi** (open in the mornings and afternoons and closed on Mondays) displays, under dimmed lighting, eight magnificent 16th-century **Flemish tapestries** in a fine state of preservation.

The excavations of **Lilybaeum** are located on Capo Boeo (open from Monday to Saturday in the mornings and afternoons) and are just a short walk from the centre. The **Museo Archeologico di Baglio Anselmi**, located in a former marsala distillery, houses a fine collection of works from Punic to Roman times.

Mazara del Vallo *

An important harbour under the **Phoenicians**, a busy port under the **Greeks** and an active trading post for the Africans, Mazara del Vallo has a long history and a colourful profile. Even today many of its inhabitants are Tunisian by origin and the **Tunisian district**, just behind the fishing port, is

> **GARIBALDI'S LANDING**
>
> On 11 May 1860, Garibaldi and his group of 1000 '**red-shirts**' landed at **Marsala**. The premier wine producer, Florio, relates how the freedom fighter landed unopposed in the port and marched into Florio's to **sample some of their marsala**. Once they had finished their drink, they set off and left behind a cache of weapons, which are on display today. You can visit Florio, by appointment (tel: 0903 781111), see the cellars and **Garibaldi's weapons**, and sample a glass of the town's famous marsala wine.

Below: *The interior of the fine Baroque cathedral in Mazara del Vallo.*

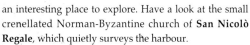

THE DEATH OF AESCHYLUS

Aeschylus was a great **Greek tragic dramatist** who wrote more than 80 plays. He transformed the conventions of theatre by introducing a second actor and creating dialogue and action independent of the chorus. He met his death in Sicily in very unusual circumstances. According to legend, Aeschylus was killed when an eagle dropped a tortoise onto his bald head, mistaking it for a stone.

an interesting place to explore. Have a look at the small crenellated Norman-Byzantine church of **San Nicolò Regale**, which quietly surveys the harbour.

The town's largely Baroque **Cathedral** was originally built during Norman times, but has been considerably restored and remodelled. The **Piazza della Repubblica**, behind the cathedral, represents the old medieval part of town. There are a number of exquisite buildings, such as the **Palazzo Episcopale** and the **Seminario**. For a pleasant stroll along the seafront, head for the **Lungomare Mazzini**.

Selinunte **

This is another beautiful site; largely untouched Greek remains protrude from a blanket of weeds and flowers.

Founded in the 7th century BC by the inhabitants of Megara Hyblaea, and basking in prosperity for two centuries, the city of Selinunte spreads out along the coast. It covers a large area, so be prepared to walk if you want to see it all, and bring along a picnic basket so that you can give the ruins the time they deserve.

The name Selinunte derives from the Greek word *selinon* (wild celery), which grows profusely here. The

heyday for Selinunte was in the 5th century BC when the city expanded and was laid out in an extensive rectilinear form. From this illustrious era we now see the **Templi Orientali**, a series of fragmented temples identified only by letters. Doric **Temple E** was probably dedicated to Hera, the ruined and smaller **Temple F** was possibly dedicated to Athena, while the huge **Temple G** may have been dedicated to Jupiter, but it is not known whether or not this impressive building was ever completed.

The **Acropolis**, a kilometre away beyond where the port used to be, houses various temples (Temple A and O) constructed in the early part of the 5th century BC. **Temple C**, on the highest point of the hill, is seemingly the oldest temple of all (dating from the early 6th century BC) and probably dedicated to Apollo.

Further afield lies the **Sanctuario della Malophoros**, a sacred area dedicated to Demeter Malophoros, goddess of vegetation and therefore the protector of the agricultural community. Interestingly, many terracotta figurines have been unearthed near another sacred area, dedicated to Zeus Meilichios, also not far away.

Cave di Cusa *

An unusual and interesting side trip just 18km (11 miles) away leads to the Cave di Cusa, which are the **ancient quarries** from which the stone for building Selinunte was hewn. It is a wild spot where plants, trees and birdsong have replaced the toil of man and it has been left in the same state since work was interrupted 2500 years ago. No one really knows why these quarries were abandoned. We can see that Temple G was constructed with this stone and we can imagine that the carved stone drums still awaiting transport were destined for this same temple. There is a lot to learn about the ingenuity of a people who had yet to invent machines to facilitate the technique of stone masonry.

Castelvetrano *

It is in Castelvetrano, just 11km (7 miles) from Selinunte, where the archaeological remains from Selinunte are exhibited. The small **Museo Civico** (Via Garibaldi, open every morning and late afternoon except Sunday afternoons) has a number of interesting items including the famous bronze statue of a young man, known as the *Ephebus of Selinunte*, dating from the 5th century BC. It was stolen from a bank in 1960, later retrieved, and is now on display for all to see. The museum is very well planned and it has, among its other exhibits, a collection of bronzes, coins, votive statuettes and terracotta items.

Above: *The Cave di Cusa quarries were the source of Selinunte's building stone.* **Opposite:** *Largely overrun by nature, the vast temple complex at Selinunte has a tranquil ambience.*

MARINELLA

Just a few kilometres down the road from the entrance to Selinunte's ruins lies one of the more attractive beach resorts on the west coast. Marinella tends to get a little crowded with tourists in high season, but for the rest of the year this little **fishing village** is a charming place to base yourself. Ruins and archaeological items can be viewed nearby; the beaches are good and day trips to Segesta, Trapani and Agrigento are all convenient if you have a car.

Western Sicily at a Glance

This part is possibly the warmest, but when winter winds and rains come, it is not as protected as the east coast. It is hot and dry in **summer** and hotels in the cities remain open throughout the year. **Spring** is normally an excellent time to visit, as the profusion of wild flowers enlivens the landscape. **Autumn** often remains warmer for longer than destinations in the mainland. **Winter** is a mixture of showers and bright, warm, sunny days, but the area is blissfully uncrowded.

The **international airports** are in **Palermo** (Falcone Borsellino Airport, tel: 091 6019111 for domestic flights and tel: 091 591275 for international flights) and **Catania** (Fontanarossa Airport, tel: 095 349837/1654). Palermo is generally the better option for travelling to and around Trapani and Agrigento.

The fastest and most convenient way to travel is by **hired car**. These are available on arrival at Palermo and Catania airports.
Regular **bus services** link the main airports and the city centres of Palermo, Catania and Siracusa to Trapani (2hr from Palermo), Segesta (1hr from Palermo) and Agrigento

(2hr from Palermo and just under 3hr from Catania). Contact Autoservizi Lumia, tel: 0922 20414, for destinations east of Trapani; Autoservizi Segesta, Trapani, tel: 0923 21754, for transport to Palermo airport and city; AST, Trapani, tel: 0923 21021, for buses in Trapani province; and Autoservizi Tarantola, tel: 0924 31020 for buses to Segesta.
A **railway line** passes through Trapani, Segesta, Marsala, Mazaro and Castelvetrano. It is a slow way to travel, but relatively comfortable. For information concerning time schedules tel: 1478 88088 (toll free). Details of all railway services can be found (also in English) on website: www.fs-on-line.com Transport to the Egadi Islands is by air from Palermo and Trapani's Birgi Airport (information from Air Sicilia, tel: 0923 841423, or Gandalf Airlines, tel: 0923 842502). There are some 11 daily **sailings** in the summer from Trapani to the nearby Levanzo and Favignana and the more distant Marettimo, either by the fast hydrofoil or by the slower, less expensive, ferry (15–60min, depending on the type of vessel and the island). From Trapani there are also daily departures to Pantelleria (1-6hr, depending on the speed of vessel). There are daily departures from Marsala (2hr and 15min) to

Pantelleria. Contact Siremar, Trapani, tel: 0923 540515 (for ferries) or tel: 0923 27780 (for hydrofoils); Tirrenia (transport to Tunisia), Trapani, tel: 0923 21896; and Ustica Lines (hydrofoils and transport to Tunisia and Naples), Trapani, tel: 0923 22200.

LUXURY
Hotel Crystal, via S. Giovanni Bosco 17, Trapani, tel: 0923 20000, fax: 0923 25555, e-mail: crystal@famon-hotels.it Modern hotel, behind station.
Hotel Capo San Vito, Via Principe Tommaso, San Vito lo Capo, tel: 0923 972122, fax: 0923 972559. Most expensive hotel on edge of beach.
Approdo di Ulisse, Cala Grande, Favignana, tel: 0923 921380, fax: 0923 921511. Overpriced in season, but good facilities.
Club Village Punta Fram, Punta Fram, Pantelleria, tel: 0923 918075, fax: 0923 918244. Good facilities in this western resort just 5km (3 miles) from Porto Pantelleria.

MID-RANGE
Albergo Maccotta, via degli Argentieri 4, Trapani, tel: 0923 28418, fax: 0923 437693. Comfortable and central. Behind tourist office.
Hotel Elimo, via Vittorio Emanuele 75, Erice, tel: 0923 869377, fax: 0923 869252. Hotel in the heart of the town with views. Good restaurant.

Western Sicily at a Glance

President, via Nino Bixio 1, Marsala, tel: 0923 999333, fax: 0923 999115. Comfortable hotel, best option.
Hotel Garzia, via Piagafetta, Marinella di Selinunte, tel: 0924 46660, fax: 0924 46196. A good coastal base for travelling.

BUDGET
Albergo Moderno, via Ten Genovese 20, Trapani, tel: 0923 21247, fax: 0923 23348. A fine central address.
Hotel Pensione Messina, corso Vittorio Emanuele 71, Trapani, tel: 0923 21198. An unpretentious establishment in the centre of town.
Costa Gaia, via Savoia 123, San Vito Lo Capo, tel: 0923 972268. Inexpensive, clean and modern, on main street.
Casa San Cataldo, via Sales 23, Erice, tel: 0923 869297. Small hotel in former convent. Simple and clean.
Hotel Miraspiaggia, via Lungomare 44, San Vito Lo Capo, tel: 0923 972355, fax: 0923 972009.Simple, clean hotel on beachfront.

WHERE TO EAT

MID-RANGE
Taverno Paradiso, Lungomare Dante Alighieri, Trapani, tel: 0923 22303. On the seafront and near the fish market. An excellent restaurant. Bookings advised.
Monte San Giuliano, vicolo San Rocco 7, Erice, tel: 0923 869390. Dine on the terrace

in summer, great atmosphere.
Thàam, via Duca degli Abruzzi 32, San Vito lo Capo, tel: 0923 972836. African cuisine meets Sicilian fare in this good restaurant.
Delfino, Lungomare Mediterraneo, Marsala, tel: 0923 999565. South of city. Seafood specialities, prices between mid-range and luxury.
Il Pescatore, via Castelvetrano 191, Mazara del Vallo, tel: 0923 947580. Specializing in fish.
I Mulini, via Kania 12, Tracino (13km or 8 miles from Porto Pantelleria), Pantelleria, tel: 0923 915398. In a converted windmill – delightful! Open only in season.

BUDGET
Ristorante da Bettina, via San Cristoforo 5/7, Trapani, tel: 0923 20050. Inexpensive restaurant near port, known for its fish couscous.
La Pentolaccia, via Guarnotti 17, Erice, tel: 0923 869099. Small, pretty and well run.
Pizzeria-Ristorante Capo Lilybeo, Lungomare Bœo 40, Marsala, tel: 0923 712881. Choice of inexpensive pizzeria

and more expensive restaurant in renovated wine cellar.
Lido Azzurro-Baffo's, Marinella di Selinunte, tel: 0924 46211. On the shore, large, but inexpensive.

SHOPPING

For those who love **coral jewellery** and decorative items, Trapani is the place to shop. Erice is known for its multi-coloured **cotton rugs**. Marsala is the centre for sweet **dessert wine**.

USEFUL CONTACTS

Ufficio di Turismo, via San Francesco d'Assisi 25, Trapani, tel: 0923 545516, website: www.cinet.it/apt
Ufficio di Turismo, viale Conte Pepoli 11, Erice, tel: 0923 869388.
Ufficio di Turismo, Via Savoia, San Vito Lo Capo, tel: 0923 972464. Open only in season.
Ufficio di Turismo, via 11 Maggio 100, Marsala, tel: 0923 714097.
Ufficio di Turismo, piazza Sta Veneranda 2, Mazara del Vallo, tel: 0923 941727 (open mornings only).

TRAPANI	J	F	M	A	M	J	J	A	S	O	N	D
AVERAGE TEMP. °F	53	54	55	59	65	72	77	78	74	68	60	56
AVERAGE TEMP. °C	12	12	13	15	18	22	25	26	23	20	16	13
HOURS OF SUN DAILY	4	4	5	7	8	10	10	10	8	6	5	4
RAINFALL in	2.4	2.1	2.4	1.9	0.9	0.5	0.1	0.4	1.8	2.4	2.6	2.4
RAINFALL mm	61	53	61	48	23	13	3	10	46	61	66	61
DAYS OF RAINFALL	9	7	5	5	3	2	1	1	5	7	7	9

4
Southern Central Sicily

Were it not for the magnificent temples in Agrigento, half the visitors to Sicily might never explore this region, for the southern central area of the island was always considered remote, slightly forbidding and the stronghold of the lawless. It embraces large parts of three fascinating provinces: Agrigento, Enna and Caltanissetta. With the fast highway from Palermo to Catania slicing through the central mountains, access to this area has become simple and convenient, and the route to Enna or Caltanissetta is a lot easier than the route to Agrigento itself.

Agrigento is a highlight of any Sicilian trip. Its history and temples place it among the most prestigious sites in Italy and the visitor should give it the time that it deserves, visiting the ruins at quieter periods of the day when, with a little imagination, its ancient columns speak of headier times.

There is yet more ancient history in this large region. Coastal **Eraclea Minoa** sits on a divine site, ancient **Gela** has a superb archaeological museum while the overgrown ruins at **Morgantina** bring a delightful tranquillity to this once-prosperous Greek site. Another highlight of those classical days is the fabulous mosaic-work in the **Villa Casale**, near **Piazza Armerina**. Within the mountains, the provincial capitals of **Enna** and **Caltanissetta**, and the ceramic-producing town of **Caltigirone**, have the advantage of great scenery and few tourists – and yet the coast is still within striking distance.

Mare Tirreno (Tyrrhenian Sea)
I. di Ustica   *Isola Eolie*
● **Palermo**
Isola Egadi   *Mare Ionio (Ionian Sea)*
Agrigento
I. di Pantelleria
Mare Mediterraneo (Mediterranian Sea)

DON'T MISS

*** Agrigento: visit its outstanding temples.
*** Villa Romana del Casale: view these spectacular mosaics.
** Museo Archeologico Regionale Agrigento: see its fine collection of Greek and Roman exhibits.
** Caltagirone: the ceramic capital of the region, with a fine museum.
* Morgantina: a dreamy Greek site, blissfully free of tourists.
* Enna: for its position and the Museo Alessi.

Opposite: *The perfectly preserved Temple of Concordia in Agrigento.*

AGRIGENTO

The provincial capital, Agrigento, is usually overshadowed on the tourist's itinerary by the magnificent Greek ruins in the Valley of the Temples situated below the citadel. Despite the modern, rather unattractive buildings to the east, the town of Agrigento merits a short detour and, with a good choice of hotels, it offers a convenient base from which to explore the archaeological sites.

Cattedrale *

Located on the Viale del Duomo, the **Cathedral** is dedicated to Saint Gerland. It is essentially a 14th-century building, though its origins date back to Norman days. It shows the architectural influences of various epochs.

Biblioteca Lucchesiana *

In 1765 the Bishop Lucchesi Palli founded this important library, which contains over 45,000 volumes and manuscripts. It is located only a few minutes' walk from the Cathedral and it is only open on Friday mornings.

Lovers of **Giacomo Serpotta**'s work should also head for the church and monastery of **Santo Spirito** where he executed some fine stuccos. Note the rare Gothic portal. More Serpotta work can be seen in nearby **San Lorenzo**.

There is a panoramic view over the archaeological site from the Viale della Vittoria. The viale is located on what was once the acropolis of the Greek city **Akragas** (named after the river of the same name). It became Agrigentum under the Romans. The beauty of the ancient city was known far and wide, cited in poetry and quoted in history.

It is thought that Akragas was originally founded around 580BC, as a colony of Gela (*see* page 75). The city was governed by a series of tyrants, the cruelest of which was Phalaris. Some 60 years later Theron, a sage ruler, captured the town of Himera. He was instrumental in extending the influence of Akragas and defeating the Carthaginians. It is thought that over 200,000 people lived in the town at that time. The Carthaginians took their revenge in 406BC and burned Agrigento. The Romans finally succeeded in taking the city in 210BC and it remained part of the Empire until its downfall. Ruins of this ancient city (including the 2300-year-old **Hereon's tomb**) are open to visitors.

Valle dei Templi ★★★

Rising above the olive trees and yellow broom, the 10 temples that were constructed between the 6th and 5th centuries BC have largely subsided into ruins. The cause was probably a mixture of seismic activity and Christian destruction. However, the magnificent **Tempio della Concordia** escaped destruction, because it was converted into a church in the 6th century. Some of the stone was purloined for later buildings and what is left today is largely ruins in a magnificent field of flowers and trees. The site is open daily and the museum is open every morning and Tuesday to Saturday afternoons.

THE PUNIC WARS

When the Phoenicians were conquered by the Assyrians in the 6th century BC, the powerful Phoenician-founded city of Carthage remained an independent state. From this time it began expanding and extending its control across North Africa and into Spain. With the rise of the Roman Empire in the middle of the 3rd century BC (Rome controlled the toe of Italy and Carthage held the west of Sicily), clashes were inevitable and the **First Punic War** was fought between 264 and 241BC. Between 218 and 201BC, the Carthaginians waged the **Second Punic War** (during which time Carthaginian Hannibal crossed the Alps). For half a century there was an uneasy peace, but between 149 and 146BC, the **Third Punic War** took place, ending when Rome destroyed Carthage.

Left: *The Valley of the Temples in Agrigento is one of Italy's finest temple complexes.*

Opposite: *The beautiful
and renowned statue of
Ephebus, Museo Regionale
Archeologico, Agrigento.*
Below: *Tempio di Junone
(or Juno), Agrigento.*

The visit begins near the major temples along Via
Sacra. The **Tempio d'Ercole** (Temple of Hercules) is
the oldest of the Doric buildings. Only a few columns
stand above the crumbling stone ruins and these were
re-erected in the 1920s by Englishman Alexander
Hardcastle who took much interest in the excavation of
Agrigento. It is hard to visualize this temple, but there is
something appealing in its solitary columns.

Nearby is the **Tempio di Giove**, or the Temple of
Jupiter (the god's Greek name is Zeus), which is an
unfinished Doric temple that stands at 110 x 53m (37 x
17.5yd). It would have been one of the Ancient World's
largest temples. Its construction called for 38 columns –
14 located along the long walls and seven along the
shorter ones – rounded on the exterior, flat on the interi-
or and joined together to form a corrugated wall. In
between these 38, *atlantes* (or *telamones*, giant figures)
were destined to be erected. A replica of the only surviving *telamon* lies on his back as it was found on the site.
The word derives from the Greek, meaning a support,
and in the museum you can see the original giant and
the ways archaeologists believe they were used.

It requires far less imagination to visualize the smaller **Tempio della Concordia** as it had been on completion in 440BC. Thirty-four columns form its peristyle, while the pediment is supported by an alternation of triglyphs and plain metopes. The harmony of this monument is due, in part, to the architectural distortions intentionally effected so that the normal optical distortions with distance and height are counterbalanced. These are intriguing Greek inventions and their modifications heightened the appearance of perfect architectural symmetry.

The Temple of Juno (the Italians prefer Tempio di Junone), or the **Tempio di Hera Lacinia** (the goddess's Greek name), stands apart from the rest of the temples at the far end of the Via Sacra and offers magnificent, energetic views. It, too, is in ruins having been torched by the Carthaginians in 406BC. It had a short life, being erected only 44 years prior to this. It had 34 columns of which a few have fallen and the rest are in a poor state of repair.

Other monuments worth visiting are the sanctuaries to the west of the Temple of Jupiter, including the **Sanctuario delle Divinità Ctonie**. This building is wrongly known as the Tempio dei Dioscuri (the brothers Castor and Pollux). This latter ruin is a 19th-century reconstruction of various elements from different monuments and although it is pretty, it is not authentic. Two columns remain from the **Tempio Efesto**. The **Casa Pace** houses the **Antiquarium di Agrigento Palaeocristiana**, which documents the early Christian use of the site.

Museo Regionale Archeologico ★★★

This superb museum is not to be missed. It is located in the part of the monastery attached to the 13th-century church of **San Nicolà**, which accommodates splendid carved marble sarcophagi.

ISOLA DI LAMPEDUSA

Lampedusa (part of the Pelagian Islands and nearer to Tunisia than Sicily) is a small 21km² (8 square mile) of rocky limestone, which rises 133m (436ft) above sea level. It boasts prehistoric, Punic and Roman remains, but is better known today as a fine and **tranquil retreat** for sun and sea lovers. It is particularly rich in **marine life** (the surrounding waters are deep) and **turtles** come ashore to lay their eggs. Some 40km (25 miles) to the north, the smaller island of **Linosa** is a fertile volcanic drop in the mediterranean Sea. The third islet, **Lampione**, is uninhabited. Lampedusa is reached by boat from Agrigento (Via Linosa) and by plane from Palermo.

Among the most impressive exhibits are the beautiful *Ephebus of Agrigento* (a marble statue, discovered in a well, of a near perfect youth dating from the 5th century BC), the sole, gigantic *telamon* that was found in the Tempio di Giove, a magnificent collection of **decorated vases, terracotta figurines** found in the sanctuaries, an amphora and painted kraters (vases with a pair of handles on the neck) – all dating from the height of the Greek Empire.

FURTHER AFIELD FROM AGRIGENTO

Luigi Pirandello was born in **Caos**, very close to Agrigento, in 1867 and a small museum (open mornings and afternoons) commemorates this great Italian writer with a collection of documents, family photographs and personal objects. His ashes were interred here at his request.

The small town of **Naro**, possibly established in Greek times, witnessed the decline of most successive powers. Its enduring legacy is, however, the **Norman Duomo** and its impressive portals. Frederick II of Swabia used the town as a royal retreat and as a result there was a proliferation of **Baroque palaces and churches**.

The Prince of Lampedusa, ancestor of Giuseppe Tomasi di Lampedusa, the author of *Il Gattopardo* (The Leopard), founded Palma di Montechiaro in the 17th century. It has subsequently declined into a poor and dusty town amid almonds, olives and vineyards.

Eraclea Minoa *

On the road between Agrigento and Sciacca and at the mouth of the River Platani (known as the Halykos to the Ancient Greeks) lie the ruins of Greek Eraclea Minoa. Once again the site is magnificent – an isolated hill with an expansive sweep of turquoise sea and chalky white cliffs and, below this, the white sandy beach of **Capo Bianco**. A visit to this site can easily be combined with a trip to the beach at **Montallegro Marina**, which is situated just behind the small town of Montallegro.

**LUIGI PIRANDELLO
(1867–1936)**

Pirandello (born to wealthy sulphur merchants in Agrigento) pursued studies in philosophy at universities in Rome and Bonn. His first book of verse, *Mal giocondo*, was published in 1889, but it is his short stories concerning the nature of the human personality which brought him success. Following the ruin of the sulphur business, his wife's increasing insanity and his own venture into the work field, he published *The Late Mattia Pascal* (often acclaimed as his best work). His *Six Characters in Search of an Author* was published in 1921, **Henry IV** in 1922, and he also wrote over 50 plays. In 1934 he received the **Nobel Prize for Literature**. He died in Paris at the age of 69.

This Greek town, probably another of Selinunte's colonies, was founded in the 6th century BC. The Romans subsequently claimed it in the 3rd century. The excavations reveal city walls, brick houses with fragments of **mosaics** and the remains of a **theatre**. The small **museum** has a few pieces including material from the necropolis.

Sciacca *

Further west along the road to Trapani you'll come to Sciacca. It was well known to the Romans as a place to relax in thermal waters and it was later a place favoured by the Normans. The Arabic and European influences explain its long reputation for producing ceramics, while the multicoloured houses around the port and the fleets of pleasure craft express this fusion. Sciacca is known for its colourful carnival celebrations.

The **Piazza Scandaliato**, considered the heart of town, offers panoramic views from its terrace over the lower port and sea. It is connected to the **Piazza del Duomo**. The **Duomo** harbours sculptures by members of the **Gagini family** and although it was founded in Norman times, it was remodelled in the mid-17th century. Items collected by Francesco Scaglione are now exhibited in his former home, the **Palazzo Scaglione** (open Monday, Tuesday and Thursday mornings and Tuesday and Thursday afternoons). These include paintings, sculptures, coins and encyclopedias.

Moving westward you will see the unusual façade of **Palazzo Steripinto**. It is a palace with protruding pyramid-shaped blocks. Pollution has sadly discoloured the lower parts. One of the sculpted portals of the former church of **Santa Margherita** is also worth looking at. **Francesco Laurana** executed it in 1468 and it has recently been cleaned.

ERACLEA MINOA

The name of this Greek settlement may possibly have been taken from the Cretan king, **Minos**. According to legend, he pursued **Daedelus** in order to punish him for helping **Ariadne** (his daughter) and Theseus escape the Labyrinth. Minos was killed by **Cocalo** and, according to the writer Diodorus, his bones were found by **Theron Akragas** (ruler of Agrigento) at the spot now called Minoa.

Opposite: *Eraclea Minoa commands a beautiful position above the south coast of Sicily.*
Below: *The thermal baths in Sciacca, used for both medicinal and recreational purposes.*

Below: *Sicily produces a wide range of interesting and often vibrant pottery.*

Thermal Baths *

The inhabitants of Selinunte used the thermae along this coast both for pleasure and for medicinal reasons. The **sulphurous water** and **mud baths** have proved to be effective in the relief of arthritis, osteo-arthritis and the treatment of skin diseases. The large thermal establishment of **Nuove Terme**, built in a distinctive Liberty style, has been renovated and offers a full range of treatments such as mud baths and vapour cleansing. The **Piscina Molinelli** offers the chance to swim in curative waters.

There are some beautiful mountains behind the coast that afford fine excursions. The 386m (1266ft) **Mount Kronio** (also called Mount San Calogero) was known in ancient times as the refuge of Daedelus, but today's visitors are oblivious to the Ancients' legends for they come to admire the panorama. Through curiosity they inspect the **Sanctuario de San Calogero** (where there is a statue of the saint by Giacomo Gagini) on the summit. Thermal vapours still escape the hillside and fill some of the caves, giving the mountain a reputation for healing, and there is even a small spa here. The **Stufe di San Calogero** is the best-known of these thermal caves and has been in use since the Bronze Age.

Caltanissetta *

The capital and the province share the same name – which means the rock of women – and this small capital does not usually attract foreigners. The province is said to have a reputation as home to various families involved in the Mafia. It knew greater prosperity a century ago when renowned for its production of sulphur, but this is now eclipsed by American companies.

Left: *Rural life has changed little over the centuries and it is not unusual to meet locals travelling on donkeys and mules.*

The handsome, twin-towered **Duomo** was built in 1570, but its interior was completed later. Among the highlights of the light and airy gilt interior are the 18th-century paintings in the vault by **Guglielmo Borremans**. The church of **San Sebastiano** lies opposite the cathedral and is recognizable by its red façade and blue belfry.

Archaeology buffs head for the **Museo Civico** (open mornings and afternoons), a museum with a fine archaeological collection amassed from sites throughout the province. The most interesting items include pieces from the **Greek necropolis** at Gibil-Gabib, such as vases and kraters, and pieces from the Bronze Age village of **Sabucina** – you can visit the site some 12km (8 miles) east of Caltanissetta – which was later occupied by the Greeks. The **Abbazia di Santo Spirito**, outside the town, is an interesting Norman basilica founded by Roger I in the middle of the 11th century.

GELA

The city and port of Gela, founded some 2600 years ago by a colony of Cretans, knew considerable prosperity and indeed it was from Gela that the city of Agrigento

---

LAGO DESUERI

Lost in the hills due east of Buteri, in the province of Caltanissetta, is Lake Desueri, which is actually a reservoir. It is known for the prehistoric tombs which have been unearthed around the lake, throwing light on the era of Sicily's early history.

was founded. Today, it is a large town of little appeal with an extended waterfront and a few interesting sights from the classical world. They are all interspersed between ugly, half-finished contemporary buildings. On a literary note, the poet Aeschylus died in **Gela** in 456BC (*see* panel, page 63).

Above: *The hilltop town of Calascibetta, viewed from Enna.*

Museo Archeologico Regionale **

This is one of the most interesting museums in Sicily. It is open each morning and afternoon and it is well organized, easy to follow and boasts some remarkable offerings. Among these are a collection of **amphorae**, which feature the ancient port's important role in trade; items from the **acropolis** (the antefixes' unsightly little faces are particularly interesting), and a cache of silver coins which were minted in both Ancient Greece and Sicily. The museum houses one of the finest collections of terracotta pottery in Italy.

The **fortifications** in the western part of the town (Capo Soprano) are also worth a visit since the ancient Greek sandstone walls, which were engulfed in sand for centuries before excavation, are in particularly good condition. They are still sturdy, though 2400 years old, and extend nearly 300m (1000ft). Later construction included **brick towers** and you can see the remains of an old **kiln**.

Enna **

A town where clouds frequently obscure the views, Enna is often isolated from its surroundings. The inhabitants of Enna are reputed to have aloof attitudes and each family frequents its own district and parish church, but Enna is an interesting place and it merits a visit for its many beautiful **churches**. It is the smallest main provincial town in Sicily and serves as a good place to centre oneself for visits around the area. The town is situated on top of a hill and offers fabulous views of the surrounding countryside including a fine view of the **Calascibetta** settlement. It is crowned by a rather imposing castle – said to be best medieval fortress on the island – which once had 20 towers. The castle provides a better sight for its exterior than its ruined interior. Frederick III of Aragon adopted the **Castello di Lombardia** (open daily) as his residence in 1324.

The **Duomo** was founded at the beginning of the 14th century, but only the apse and the transepts have survived the years. Much of the building, dating from the 16th century, is Baroque in appearance. The dark columns and their unusual carved bases are the work of a number of sculptors including Gian Domenico Gagini.

One of Enna's memorable features is the **Museo Alessi** (open in the mornings and afternoons, but closed on Mondays), which is situated just behind the Duomo. This collection, once the property of Canon Alessi (1774–1837), contains bejewelled **silver treasures** from the Duomo archaeological finds, and a superb **collection of coins**. The exhibits are displayed well, which makes it a pleasure to explore the collection. Lastly, the **Museo Archeologico** has a collection of material found on classical sites in the surrounding area.

PIAZZA ARMERINA

The hilltop town of Piazza Armerina, in the province of Enna, is often overlooked in favour of the nearby classical sites, yet the town has an interesting medieval centre and fine buildings. The most significant event of the year, **Palio dei Normanni**, is celebrated on 13 and 14 August. This is when the **Piazza del Duomo** shrugs off the 21st century and

---

LAKE PERGUSA

For over 35 years, Enna's Pergusa used to host the annual international **Formula 3000** at its racetrack. This unique oval circuit follows the shore of Lake Pergusa, the island's only natural lake, which is roughly only 5m (16.4ft) deep. Today, it has become a conservation area as the pine forests hide a wealth of both migratory and resident birds. An odd type of micro-organism is responsible for turning the lake waters red each decade or so. Nearby **Cozze Matrice** is the site of a preclassical settlement where there are remains of Bronze Age huts and a necropolis.

Below: *A gracious town, Piazza Armerina has both Norman and Baroque buildings.*

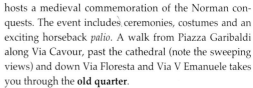

THE LAST QUEEN OF SICILY

Until some 78 years ago, Sicily still had a queen. Daughter of Maximilian, Duke of Bavaria, **Maria Sophia** married **Francesco**, Duke of Calabria (later to become King of Two Sicilies) in 1859 while her elder sister, 'Sissi', married the emperor Frans Joseph I of Austria. However, when Vittorio Emanuele II, King Francesco's cousin, was made **King of Italy** in 1861, the Sicilian royal couple were **exiled** to Rome. Francesco died in 1894 while his widowed queen lived the rest of her life between Paris and Munich. She died in 1925 and was buried in Naples.

hosts a medieval commemoration of the Norman conquests. The event includes ceremonies, costumes and an exciting horseback *palio*. A walk from Piazza Garibaldi along Via Cavour, past the cathedral (note the sweeping views) and down Via Floresta and Via V Emanuele takes you through the **old quarter**.

The **Duomo** crowns the medieval part of the town, but it is, in fact, a Baroque masterpiece. It is a building with a graceful, light and airy interior and the blue and white colour scheme is tranquil. The painting in the large silver frame is a copy of the Byzantine *Madonna della Victoria* (said to have been given to Count Roger by the Pope). The Gagini family was responsible for the arcade under which you'll find the **baptismal font**.

Villa Romana del Casale ***

This luxurious villa, located just a couple of kilometres outside the town and nestling in the valley at Casale, is one of Sicily's most remarkable sights. Although it was

occupied until the 12th century, the villa lay largely undiscovered under the rubble of a landslide until concerted conservation efforts under Vinicio Gentili brought the whole area to attention in the 1950s.

It was built between the 3rd and 4th centuries AD for an unknown patron. Educated guesses identify the owner as **Maximian**, one of Rome's wealthiest citizens and co-emperors. However, what is incontestable is the extraordinary legacy of **coloured mosaics**, 3500m² (4180 square yard) in total, that 'carpet' the floors and give us an extraordinary insight into Roman life, costumes and customs over 1700 years ago. Unfortunately the dust and dirt which blow in through the permanently open doors do little justice to their wonderful colours, but there are fine photos in the numerous guide books on sale outside the Villa.

The visit begins in the **thermae** (the bathing area) and progresses through the octagonal **frigidarium** and into the oval **Sala del Circo** (which was probably used as a gymnasium). There are about a dozen little rooms through which one passes – mostly by way of an elevated ramp so that the mosaics are protected – until you reach

the extraordinary **Sala delle Dieci Ragazze**, which never fails to amuse. Here is a mosaic portraying 10 girls working out as one would expect in a modern-day gym – the notion that the bikini was invented on the French Riviera is proved a myth.

Nearby the **Sala della Piccola Caccia** is another marvellous scene of hunters and their prey. One picture illustrates a heavy boar being transported in a net while a hunting dog is attacking it and the hunter is trying to protect his prey by fending off the dog with a spear.

The 64m (215ft) **Ambulacro della Grande Caccia** is an indulgence of fabulous mosaic work. It is surely one of the most spectacular ever found in the Roman world. It shows a series of hunting scenes and depicts an obvious portrait of a dignitary, possibly Maximian, flanked by two guards. There are galleys, exotic fish, African beasts and a veritable array of wild animals all accomplished with remarkable accuracy. There are many more interesting rooms including the triclinium, with its *Labours of Hercules*, and a room of erotic portrayals.

Morgantina ★★★

This Greek town is located about 16km (10 miles) northeast of Piazza Armerina. It is a fascinating site (open mornings and afternoons) and it is enhanced by its beautiful location, a profusion of wild flowers and the fact that not too many visitors tramp around the ruins.

Above: *The ruins of Morgantina are cloaked in wild flowers.*
Opposite: *A series of raised walkways enables visitors to admire the mosaics at Villa Romana del Casale.*

THE ROMAN GODS

Bacchus – god of wine
Ceres – goddess of tillage and corn
Diana – goddess of light and hunting
Juno – wife of Jupiter
Jupiter – chief among the Roman gods
Mars – god of war
Mercury – god of merchandise, theft and eloquence
Minerva – goddess of wisdom
Neptune – god of the sea
Saturn – god of agriculture
Venus – goddess of love
Vesta – goddess of hearth and household
Vulcan – god of fire and metalworking

Excavations began in the 1950s (by archaeologists from Princeton University) and a town, which had its heyday in the 2nd century BC, was unearthed. They found an **agora**, a small **theatre**, a public **granary** (beside which is a covered **brick kiln**), remains of a sanctuary and a temple and, on the eastern hillside above the commercial centre of the Greek town, the remains of an early **Siculi settlement** (dating ca. 1000BC). The Greeks sited their acropolis on this and you'll find the remains of **mosaics** (the oldest known in the Hellenistic world) in the so-called **Casa di Ganimede**, while the **Casa del Capitello Dorico** is named for the Doric column which has survived the house.

Caltagirone ***

Visitors often neglect Caltagirone (part of Catania province) since it lies a way off the usual routes to Palermo, Agrigento or Siracusa. It is more easily accessible from the provincial capitals of Ragusa, Caltanissetta and Enna and it has a lot to offer.

THE GREEK TOWN

Although the Greek town centre was similar in function to the later Roman one, there are various features to look out for:

Agora: the open market-place or gathering place akin to a main square
Bouleuterion: court or council chamber
Ekklesiasterion: place of public assembly
Gymnasium: the public health club of the day
Macellum: slaughterhouse and market stalls
Prytaneion: town hall
Stoa: colonnaded path or portico
Theatre: a hemispherical raked theatre

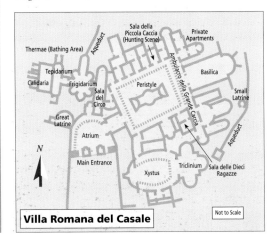

Villa Romana del Casale

Labels on map: Sala della Piccola Caccia (Hunting Scene); Private Apartments; Thermae (Bathing Area); Aqueduct; Tepidarium; Calidaria; Frigidarium; Sala del Circo; Peristyle; Ambulacro della Grande Caccia; Basilica; Small Latrine; Great Latrine; Atrium; N; Main Entrance; Xystus; Triclinium; Sala delle Dieci Ragazze; Aqueduct; Not to Scale

It is obvious on arrival that Caltagirone is known for its **ceramics**. It is an average-sized town of nearly 40,000 inhabitants and it has over 100 ceramic workshops and factories producing household goods and ornaments (plates, vases and decorative items) as well as architectural elements (façades and balconies). Reminders of its industry pervade the whole town, from the delightful music **pergola** in the Villa Comunale **public gardens** to the tile rises between the steps of the impressive **Scala di Santa Maria del Monte** (connecting old and new Caltagirone). On the evenings of 24 and 25 July each step is illuminated with oil lamps, creating a magical scene.

Caltagirone has been producing ceramics from local clay for over 3000 years. Initiated by the Cretans, continued by the Greeks and refined by the Arabs, the characteristics of its ceramics include geometric designs and an application of yellow, blue and green.

A collection of local, and other Sicilian, ceramics produced over the last couple of millennia is effectively illustrated at the **Museo Regionale della Ceramica** (open daily). Here you'll discover terracotta heads, vases and amphorae from antiquity. The **Museo Civico** (open in the mornings from Tuesday to Sunday and in the late afternoons on Tuesday, Friday, Saturday and Sunday) is housed in **Carcere Borbonico** (once a prison). It offers a collection of more modern and contemporary ceramics.

The town converges on the Piazza Umberto I where the **Duomo di San Giuliano** is located.

> **GLI IBLEI MOUNTAINS**
>
> These mountains straddle the provincial frontier and are a centre of citrus cultivation and livestock contained by low limestone walls. Among their deep valleys, or on the hilltops, are some interesting small towns and plenty of panoramic viewpoints – the highest peak, **Mount Contessa**, tops 914m (3059ft). The town of **Grammichele**, near Caltagirone, was rebuilt on an octagonal plan after the earthquake of 1693 and the road to and from this town is particularly attractive. **Palazzolo Acreide**, with its majestic Baroque church of San Sebastiano and elegant piazza, is a very pleasant and seldom visited town (which merits more visitors). **Monterosso Almo**'s church of San Giovanni, a work attributed to Vicenzo Sinatra, is also an unusual building.

Opposite: *The rises of Caltagirone's 142-stair Scala di Santa Maria del Monte are enlivened by colourful ceramics.*
Left: *Caltagirone's ceramics are also used to decorate the town's bandstand.*

Southern Central Sicily at a Glance

BEST TIMES TO VISIT

Agrigento attracts visitors throughout the year and the site remains spectacular during all four seasons. The **winters** are cool, and sometimes rainy, and the main hotels are open during this time. Elsewhere, **springtime** is a fine time to visit. The fruit trees are in flower and later the wild flowers carpet the hills and valleys. **Summer** is very hot and crowded with local and international visitors, although the temperatures are cooler in the hills.
Autumn is a pleasant time to travel once the summer visitors and school children have returned home. Three **annual events** are worth noting: **Sciacca** holds a popular annual carnival which is much renowned.
Piazza Armerina holds its *palio* on 13 and 14 August, and **Caltanissetta** bursts into festivities for the patron saint, St Michael, at the end of September.

GETTING THERE

The nearest **airport** to Agrigento is Palermo, which is 128km (80 miles), or 90min, away. Buses run regularly from **Palermo Falcone Borsellino Airport** and the city to Agrigento. For **bus** information, contact Cammileri (tel: 0922 39084) or Cuffaro (tel: 091 6161510 or 0922 39909).
The 165km (103-mile) bus

ride from **Catania**'s **Fontanarossa** airport takes approximately 3hr. For bus information contact Catania with SAIS, tel: 095 531756. Agrigento is also on the railway line (Agrigento Centrale) and linked to Palermo (2hr).

GETTING AROUND

If you have not hired a **car** (which makes getting to the mountains and the more remote places so much easier), the bus is the best way to get around. There are routine **bus services** from Agrigento to Caltanissetta (75min) and Enna (2hr). Buses to Trapani travel via Sciacca and Eraclea Minoa while, in the opposite direction, there are buses to Gela. There are bus trips between Caltagirone or Caltanissetta and Piazza Armerina (1hr) and more frequent trips between Enna and Piazza Armerina (45–90min, depending on the route). Caltagirone is nearer to Catania than other cities and it can be reached from Catania or its airport (approximately 75min).
Railway services exist between Gela and Caltagirone and extend towards Catania. There is a winding line in the other direction, which leads to Agrigento and Palermo from Caltagirone. For details in Italian, tel: 1478 88088. English timetables are attainable at www.fs-on-line.com

WHERE TO STAY

LUXURY
Hotel Villa Athena, Via Panoramica dei Templi, Agrigento, tel: 092 596288, fax: 092 402180. Stunning temple views from this delightful average-sized hotel. Good restaurant.
Baglio della Luna, contrada Maddalusa, SS115, Agrigento, tel: 0922 511061, fax: 0922 598802. Small hotel built on an ancient farm. A hired car is recommended. Very comfortable.
Park Hotel Paradiso, contrada Ramaldo S.N., Piazza Armerina, tel: 0935 680841, fax: 0935 683391. Just outside the city, on the road towards Casale, a large, renovated hotel with full facilities and good restaurant.

MID-RANGE
Hotel Pirandello, Via Giovanni XXIII, Agrigento, tel: 0922 595666, fax: 0922 402497. Budget category out of season, in the eastern part of Agrigento.
Costazzurra, via delle Viole 2/4, San Leone, near Agrigento, tel: 0922 411222, fax: 0922 414040. Just 8km (5 miles) south of Agrigento, On the coast. A hired car is recommended.
Mosaici da Battiato, near Villa Casale, Piazza Armerina, tel/fax: 0935 685453. An alternative to staying in town, ideal for visiting the villa. Also has a very good restaurant.

Southern Central Sicily at a Glance

Hotel delle Terme, Via delle Nuove Terme, Sciacca, tel: 0925 23133, fax: 0925 87002. Comfortable hotel used primarily by those taking the waters. Good pools.

Il Gattopardo, cala Creta, Lampedusa Island, tel: 0922 970051. Reservations: Turin, tel: 011 8178385/6, fax: 011 8178387. Small hotel in villa. Tranquil paradise for sea lovers. Inclusive weekly rates.

BUDGET

Bella Napoli, piazza Lena 6, Agrigento town, tel/fax: 0922 29435. Inexpensive mid-sized hotel in heart of old town.

Fattoria Mosè, via M Pascal 4, Villaggio Mosè (4km eastwards on Gela road), Agrigento, tel/fax: 0922 606115. Just outside town. A very small, comfortable and very popular farm. Booking essential.

La Paloma Blanca, via Figuli 5, tel: 0925 25667, fax: 0925 25130. Spacious rooms in simple, clean style.

Ventura, strada Statale 640, 1.5km southwest of town, Caltanissetta, tel: 0934 553780, fax: 0934 553785. Hotel with good restaurant.

WHERE TO EAT

LUXURY

Hotel Villa Athena, (see Where To Stay)

MID-RANGE

Le Caprice, via Panoramica dei Templi 25, Agrigento, tel: 0922 26469. Excellent restaurant with views of the temples. Average prices.

Leon d'Oro, viale Emporium 112, San Leone, tel: 0922 414400. Family-run trattoria. Traditional dishes and pleasant atmosphere.

Kalo's, Piazzetta San Calogero, Agrigento town, tel: 0922 26389. One of the town's better restaurants. Near main square.

La Scala, scala Maria Santissia del Monte 8, Caltagirone, tel: 0933 57781. On the famous steps. A good restaurant with regional specialities.

Al Fogher, strada Statale 117 bis, contrada Bellia, 3km (north), Piazza Armerina, tel: 0935 684123. Excellent cuisine, but closed mid-June to mid-July.

Legumerie Le Fontanelle, via Pietro Leone 45, contrada Fontanelle, 2km northwest of Caltanissetta, tel: 0934 592437. An agroturistic venture, at edge of town. Serves excellent food (outdoors in summer).

BUDGET

Mosaici da Battiato, (see Where to Stay).

Il Pescatore, Promenade Falcone Borsellino, San Leone, tel: 0922 414342. Very popular (especially in peak season) trattoria, with a varied menu and seafood specialities.

Cortese, viale Sicilia 166, Caltanissetta, tel: 0934 591686. In the middle of town. A restaurant representing excellent value for money.

SHOPPING

Mostra Mercato Permanente, corso V Emanuele 7–9, Caltagirone, tel: 0933 56444. Permanent exhibition of many producers' ceramic wares. Excellent selection of all types of ceramics.

USEFUL CONTACTS

Ufficio di Turismo, via Cesare Battista 15, Agrigento, tel: 0922 20454.

Ufficio di Turismo, corso Vittorio Emanuele 84, Sciacca, tel: 0925 21182.

Ufficio di Turismo, via Cavour 15, Piazza Armerina, tel: 0935 680201.

Ufficio di Turismo, corso Vittorio Emanuele 109, Caltanissetta, tel: 0934 584499.

Ufficio di Turismo, via Roma 413, Enna, tel: 0935 528228.

Ufficio di Turismo, Palazzo Libertini, near Piazza Umberto I, Caltagirone, tel: 0933 53809.

GELA	J	F	M	A	M	J	J	A	S	O	N	D
AVERAGE TEMP. °F	54	54	55	58	64	70	74	76	74	68	61	56
AVERAGE TEMP. °C	17	12	12	12	14	17	23	24	23	20	16	13
DAYS OF RAINFALL	9	9	8	7	4	2	1	2	4	7	9	10

5
outheast Sicily

This southernmost part of Sicily is nearer to Malta than to mainland Italy. It looks south towards the African continent yet draws on a past that was fashioned by the Greek and Roman Empires, and the prosperous 17th and 18th centuries. The two largest towns, each a provincial capital, have their own distinct character: the port of **Siracusa** (often called Syracuse, by the English) looks back to its classical origins beyond a contemporary marina, while **Ragusa**, actually two towns separated by a saddle, breathes the elegance of its illustrious Baroque past. Another very pleasant town is the supremely Baroque Noto, where well-heeled nobility and clergy were able to rebuild the town in the then-fashionable architectural style after the catastrophic earthquake of 1693 reduced it to rubble.

Inland and beyond these towns, the quiet **Iblei Mountains** preserve a traditional, rural lifestyle where citrus and sheep characterize the rugged landscape. Southwards, the dry land slopes gently down to the coast, through areas of viticulture and market gardening which threaten to swamp its seaside villages and **tourist resorts**. Within this area there are small classical sites, a number of nature reserves (including the rather unusual **Fonte Ciane**), and small provincial towns such as **Modica** – the mighty medieval base of the Chiaramonte family with fine Baroque buildings and palm trees – or **Scicli** – the charming Baroque town rebuilt after the 1693 earthquakes – that are off the usual tourist routes and compact enough to explore with ease.

Mare Tirreno (Tyrrhenian Sea)
I. di Ustica *Isola Eolie*
Palermo
Isola Egadi *Mare Ionio (Ionian Sea)*
I. di Pantelleria *Ragusa* *Siracusa*
Mare Mediterraneo (Mediterranian Sea)

DON'T MISS

*** Siracusa: for its fine Greek theatre.
*** Noto: for its stunning Baroque architecture.
*** Ragusa Ibla: a beautiful Baroque town.
*** Museo Archeological Regionale Paolo Orsi: one of Europe's finest.
** Ortygia: a stroll through this historic part of Siracusa.
** Riserva Naturale di Vendicari: a fine sea-shore reserve.
* Siracusa Cathedral: simple yet beautiful.
* Fonte Ciane: unusual blue waters and papyrus.

Opposite: *The heart of Siracusa is its district of Ortygia.*

SIRACUSA'S ORTYGIA DISTRICT

This is an area where you should stroll slowly and absorb the centuries of history. Allow your curiosity to lead you through the narrow streets and past the Baroque homes and flower-filled balconies, for this is the soul of Siracusa, the island that once rivalled Athens itself in grandeur and elegance.

The **Corinthians** first built Ortygia in 734BC and for 500 years Siracusa prospered. It defended its independence and then its allegiance with the changing Greek colonies until it fell into Roman hands and declined in importance by the 3rd century AD. During those powerful days, luminaries such as Virgil, Aeschylus, Theocritus, Archimedes and Plato visited or lived in the city. Archimedes died here in the 3rd century BC.

Templo Apollo

A couple of columns still remain from what was one of Sicily's premier Doric buildings. The Temple of Apollo, in Largo XXV Luglio, was built from warm sandstone around 575BC. Although only little remains of it today.

Mercato *

Opposite the remains of the Temple of Apollo is the very vibrant morning market. Excellent Sicilian produce and an active early morning **fish market**

give this popular venue its commend-
able reputation. To the east of this
turn-of-the-century covered market is
a maze of narrow alleys that was once
part of the **Saracen kasbah**.

Leaving the northern part of
Ortygia past the Baroque **Piazza
Archimede** (with a fine 19th-century
fountain of Artemis by Giulio
Moschetti) you'll cross Via della
Maestranza – an elegant street, lined
with noble Baroque palazzi, which
effectively cuts Ortygia in two. It runs
between the Belvedere San Giacomo
in the east and the promenade Foro
Vittorio Emanuele II (**the Marina**) in
the west. It is lined with trees on one
side and yachts on the other.

Piazza del Duomo **

Lined by a number of gracious Baroque palazzi, this
attractive piazza was built on a foundation of Greek and
Roman ruins and it forms a focal point for the old
Siracusa. It is beautiful.

The first Christian church, taking the place of a Doric
temple dedicated to **Athena**, was erected in the 7th century and it encased the remains of Athena's temple.
Today it houses the **Duomo** (open mornings and late
afternoons). Andrea Palma's Baroque façade, designed
to replace the Norman one after the earthquake in 1693,
was added to this classical beginning. The complicated
and diverse architectural styles of this unusual cathedral
are apparent. The Baroque decoration, which once
masked the **Greek columns** of the cellar, was stripped
some 75 years ago and these columns have been incorpo-
rated into the outer walls of the aisles. The atmosphere
created is unexpectedly soothing and reverent.

Among the cathedral's treasures is the painting,
in jewel-like colours, of *St Zosimus* that was
attributed to Antonello da Messina. It can be found in

Above: *The Piazza del
Duomo is Siracusa's
Baroque centrepiece.*
Opposite: *A fountain by
Giulio Moschetti graces the
Piazza Archimede.*

SMALL PLEASURES

One of the great delights in
Siracusa is the **sunset** on a
fine day. The sun drops over
the bay and settles behind
the distant hills. Small fishing
vessels and cruisers inevitably
cross the water and head for
the harbour as night falls. To
enjoy the full spectacle, seat
yourselves at one of the
many cafés and restaurants
beyond the Marina on
Lungomare Alfeo.

the **Cappella del Crocifisso**. Look out for a silver altar and a silver statue of the Virgin in the **Cappella Santa Lucia** and admire the wrought-iron gates to the southern chapels as you enter. Saint Lucy (blinded and martyred) is the patron saint of Siracusa and there are symbolic eyes in many places. There are also a number of works by the Gagini family.

Above: *A magnificent venue for any play, the Greek theatre, Siracusa.*
Opposite: *Entrance to the mysterious cave of Dionysius's Ear.*
Below: *Papyrus grass grows in the centre of the Fonte Aretusa.*

Galleria Regionale di Palazzo Bellomo **

This palazzo, located in Via Capodieci (open in the mornings from Tuesday to Sunday), was built by the Swabian rulers at around AD1234 and then enlarged in the 15th century. It houses a number of fine medieval and Baroque exhibits including the damaged *Annunciation* by **Antonello da Messina**, the tobacco-coloured and moody *Burial of St Lucy* by **Caravaggio** (who fled to this region after escaping from a Maltese prison), a couple of works attributed to both Antonello and Domenico **Gagini**, a display outlining the history of the *presepio* (nativity scenes), and a collection of Sicilian religious and decorative art. A once refined, but now neglected, Via Roma leads you back towards the Piazza del Duomo. The opposite direction will steer you to the tip of Ortygia where the **Castello Maniace** stands. It was built in 1239 by Frederick II .

FONTE ARETUSA

This spring was famous throughout antiquity, as the Ancients believed that it was here that goddess **Arethusa** reappeared as a spring after she fled **Olympia** and the unwanted advances of a river god. The spring is also unusual in that it spouts fresh water just metres from the sea. Today, the fresh water discharges into a pond full of palms, papyrus and white ducks and it is rather more romantic than aesthetic.

SIRACUSA NEW TOWN

In stark contrast to the interesting island of Ortygia, the Siracusa to the north (modern and without charm) has little in the way of architecture to offer the tourist. The exceptions to this are the fascinating **Catacombe di San Giovanni** (a vast area of underground catacombs – the oldest in Sicily – near the remains of the **church of Santa Lucia**) and the **Sanctuario della Madonna delle Lacrime** (a modern landmark on the city skyline housing a tiny statue of the Madonna, which astounded the world with its display of tears, *see* panel, page 90).

Teatro Greco ★★★

The **largest Greek theatre** in Sicily, this hemispheric theatre with a diameter of 138m (154yd), was hewn out of the hillside and faces the sea. It is believed to have been built in the 5th century BC and it is still used for biennial performances during the early summer months.

Latomia del Paradiso ★★

These **old quarries** were responsible for providing large quantities of limestone used for both public buildings and noble homes in Siracusa. The steep-sided Latomia del Paradiso is the only one that is open to visitors and although it has an attractive feature – subtropical vegetation and fragrant trees cover the rock face and the bottom of the quarries – it also served as a prison area for thousands of Athenians.

The pointed cave known as **Dionysius's Ear** is another favourite site. This cavern was excavated out of the hillside and it was **Caravaggio** who named it. The legend tells how **Dionysius** was kept prisoner here and, because of the cave's ability to produce echoes of even the quietest sound, he was comforted by the voices of the other prisoners elsewhere in this long cavern. It still has a mysterious allure, but the echoes nowadays come from tourists testing its unusual acoustics.

Below: *Ceramics in the Museo Archeologico Regionale Paolo Orsi.*

Anfiteatro Romano *

Much of this large, 1st-century AD amphitheatre was also cut out of the hillside, which is the reason for the good state of preservation along the amphitheatre's eastern flanks. The area that was enclosed by building blocks has unfortunately not fared so well. However, the two entrances are still visible (the southern one was the principal access for spectators) and although you can't go inside the building it is still an impressive sight.

Museo Archeologico Regionale Paolo Orsi ***

It was Paolo Orsi who excavated much of southeastern Sicily's classical past (notably at Gela and Agrigento in the first decades of the 20th century) and many of the precious items he unearthed are now on display in this world-class museum (open in the mornings and afternoons from Tuesday to Saturday and on Monday afternoons). Situated in a fine garden, its layout includes three main sections: **prehistory**, **Greek colonies** (starting from the 8th century in the eastern part of Sicily) and **colonies** founded by Siracusa elsewhere on the island. There are also finds from other Hellenistic and Roman settlements on display.

The exhibits in the latter two sections of this wonderful treasury should not be missed. The revolving displays of some of the best pieces are unusual and effective.

Among the most memorable exhibits are the beautiful, but headless, marble *kouroi* from Lentinoi (a kouros is a figure of a young man); the large collection of **votives** (the equivalent of today's souvenirs available outside a religious building); the extraordinary urns dating from 2000–1500BC; a mythical fishing boat with rowers, and the unusual statue of a goddess breastfeeding twins (carved in the 6th century BC and found in Megara Hyblaea). There are many other interesting pieces that were also discovered at Megara Hyblaea, such as the headless **Venus Anadyomene** (a Roman copy of an earlier Greek

statue). It caught the attention of Guy de Maupassant when he first saw it in the 1880s and he wrote a fine description of this beautiful work.

Above: *Fontane Bianche, a popular beach resort near Siracusa.*

AROUND SIRACUSA
Fonte Ciane *

To the south of Siracusa, just 8km (5 miles) away in an area of intensive citrus culture, lies the source of the Ciane River. The spring that rises from the depths and spouts out blue, turquoise or inky waters takes its name from the Greek word *cyan*, which means blue. It is a pleasant spot (at times you may hire a boat and punt down the river) and a little further away, on the banks of the river, are the remains of an old **Doric temple** built and dedicated to Zeus in the 6th century BC. It is also possible to take a boat trip along the river and see the pretty papyrus reeds (which were supposedly a gift from Ancient Egypt), bulrushes and eucalyptus trees that flourish along the river banks.

Castello Eurialo

Approximately 9km (just over 5 miles) to the northwest of Siracusa, amid a landscape of refineries, lies the ancient Greek fortification of Castello Eurialo (open daily). It was built in 401BC by **Dionysius the Elder** and was finished some 16 years later. It is the most important extant Greek military fortification.

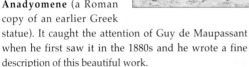

PAPYRUS

Papyrus is linked to the legend of the nymph, **Ciane**, who was turned into a spring which sprouts this plant. Papyrus is said to have been introduced to Sicily by the Greeks in the 3rd century BC, and the water-loving plant has been native to the island ever since. As with Egyptian papyrus, the plant is cultivated and used as a medium for **writing** and **painting**, although it was noted, in 250BC, that the quality of Siracusan papyrus was inferior to that of Egypt. Papyrus paper-making facilities began again in 1781 and still continue today. You can watch demonstrations of this at the **Istituto del Papiro**, via XX Settembre 19, tel: 0931 483342. A range of hand-crafted souvenirs, such as lampshades, cards and writing paper, is on sale.

Above: Delightful Baroque balconies of the huge Palazzo Nicolaci.

A LUCKY SURVIVOR

Noto's most impressive palace, the **Nicolaci di Villadorata**, was willed to a young French boy who was the only survivor of a **shipwreck**. During the French Revolution various wealthy families sought to flee France, and on one particular boat there was a noble family from Agde, Languedoc-Roussillon. The boat floundered and on observing its sinking, the **Marquis of Villadorata** sent boats to rescue the passengers. The only survivor was 7-year-old **Théodore Dejean**, who was brought up by the Marquis and, on condition he never returned to France, was left all the marquis's worldly goods. Today the descendants of Dejean live in a sumptuous villa at **San Corrado di Fuori**, which was built by the son of the first Dejean.

FURTHER AFIELD FROM SIRACUSA

The area around Siracusa is rich in sights from different eras. **Beach resorts**, such as Fontane Bianche, pepper the pretty coast south of Siracusa. The town of **Noto** has a Baroque core and one of the better beaches on the east coast at **Marina di Noto** – just 8km (5 miles) away. Behind the beach is an attractive backdrop of almond trees.

Neapolis has an archaeological museum and park with a Roman theatre, a cave and excavations (open in the afternoons during the week and Tuesday and Saturday mornings).

Noto ★★★

This is an extraordinary little town and definitely worth a visit. In a delightful Mediterranean landscape, filled with almond and olive trees and overlooking the valley carved out by the river Asinaro, Noto's elegant Baroque centre is surprising. Rebuilt after the devastating earthquake in 1693, Noto was constructed on a grid plan along three east-west roads. Two of these roads, Via Cavour and Corso Vittorio Emanuele, are lined with interesting buildings. Society was divided up into three sections and allocated accordingly: the nobility occupied the upper third, the clergy occupied the central section and the hoi polloi occupied the lower segment. Naturally, the wealthy and the clergy erected substantial **palaces** and **churches**. They chose to build with the pale, local limestone which, over the years, has taken on a peachy hue. Sicilian architects Gagliardi, Labisi and Sinatra were largely responsible for the 17th–18th-century reconstruction of Noto.

Do not miss the **Cathedral**, crowned by two fine bell towers, at the top of a majestic flight of steps (the dome and parts of the nave caved in some years ago), and the beautiful **San Francesco dell'Immacolata** (designed by **Vincenzo Sinatra**) viewed from the base of the sweeping staircase that leads upwards from the corso. Beautiful sights, next door, include the **Palazzo Landolina** and the **Palazzo Arcivescovo** (both a stone's throw away from the cathedral), the rather run-down **Palazzo Ducezio** (used as the *municipio*) and the **Palazzo Nicolaci di Villadorata** (in Via Nicolaci) with its extraordinary balconies supported by rows of prone figures of females, horses and lions.

Cava Grande *

Some 20km (12 miles) along, the road leaving Noto in the direction of Caltagirone and Enna (which winds, further on, through the pleasant Iblei Mountains) leads to the Cava Grande, which is situated on the banks of the **River Cassibile** and is now a natural reserve. The 30-minute descent to the river takes you through thick vegetation to beautiful clear pools. These are ideal spots for a dip and a picnic, but they do dry up in summer.

Riserva Naturale di Vendicari **

This pedestrian-only nature reserve, south of **Marina di Noto**, is a safe haven for migratory birds attracted to wetland areas and it is an ideal venue for lovers of nature. There are various tracks and some pleasant **beaches**, and just to the north of the reserve lies the archaeological site of **Eloro** dating from the 7th century BC. The site is perfect, since it is located on the top of a hill and faces the endless azure of the Ionian Sea, which stretches out towards Tunisia. The remains of a **theatre**, **temple** and town **walls** are all visible.

RAGUSA

Ragusa is the capital of the province which shares the same name. The city divided into the two towns of **Ragusa Superiore** and **Ragusa Ibla**. It lies in a district of stony outcrops, small-holdings separated by low stone

> **MORE RUINS**
>
> The most important site north of Siracusa is the Greek colony of **Megara Hyblaea**, which today has the most unappealing setting of large oil refineries at Augusta. Megara Hyblaea, founded in 780BC, bears necropoli, Hellenistic walls, thermal baths and a 4th-century BC Doric temple. In the Anapo valley, near Palazzolo Acreide, are **Akrai** (a 7th-century BC Greek theatre in a good state of repair) and **Pantalica** (founded in the Bronze Age and known primarily for its prehistoric hillside tombs – some 8000 in total).

Below: *Ragusa Ibla, pictured here, joins Ragusa Superiore by means of the Santa Maria delle Scale.*

CAFÉ SOCIETY

Central Sicily is a place where the men spend much time communing in the cafés (the women are at home, naturally). If you want to watch people, then take a seat at an outside table and nurse an *espresso*, a *caffè macchiato* (with a tot of milk) or a *caffè corretto* (with a tot of grappa). If it is hot, then a *birra alla spina* (a draft beer) is an acceptable drink for men, and an *aranciata* or a *succo fresco d'arancia* (fresh orange juice) is a good thirst quencher. In rural Sicily, wine is only ordered with a meal and not as an apéritif. You could ask for a marsala or malvasia. At cocktail hour, a Cinzano is always acceptable.

Opposite: *The Baroque interior of the Circolo di Conversazione.*

walls, goat and sheep rearing, and dairy produce.

Ragusa Superiore is the name given to the Baroque upper part of town built after the 1693 earthquake. Ragusa Ibla is located on a spur to the east and it is unique in having a medieval street 'plan' and Baroque buildings. Ragusa has many flights of **stairs** and wherever you turn there seems to be a flight leading upwards or downwards. There are 242 stairs in **Santa Maria delle Scale**, which lead from Ragusa Superiore to Ragusa Ibla.

Ragusa Ibla **

Not only does the town offer a fabulous panorama, but the town itself is a beautiful sight as you approach it. Like a tiered cake, houses and churches cling to the hillside and ascend toward the blue-domed Duomo of **San Giorgio** (Ragusa's *cattedrale* is in the other Ragusa). This imposing building, with its glorious Baroque façade, stands above an impressive flight of monumental stairs. It is the quintessential Sicilian Baroque church.

On the piazza in front, there is the **Circolo di Conversazione** (or Circolo dei Nobili) and the **Palazzo Donnafugata**. The first is a finely decorated conversation club (originally for the nobility, but commoners are now

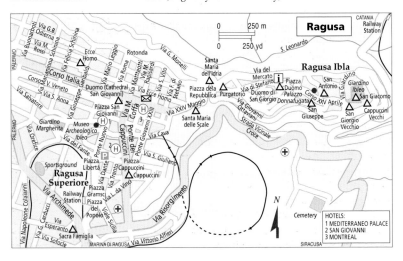

permitted and it was recently opened to women) and the second is a beautiful palace with discreet windows and a charming little wooden balcony on the upper floor allowing one to observe the activities in the square without being seen.

There are **25 churches** and chapels and a **dozen palaces** (many of which are at last being renovated) and a wander through the peaceful streets will reveal plenty of fascinating buildings.

Il Giardino Ibleo

A pretty garden situated on the eastern side of the town, the Giardino Ibleo has a fine line of palms and plenty of benches ideal for a quiet, cool picnic. Nearby lies a 15th-century Gothic portal, which is all that remains of **San Giorgio Vecchio**; the rest of the church was destroyed in the 1693 earthquake.

Ragusa Superiore **

This is one of Sicily's most elegant provincial towns. It has good shops and a fine museum, and it is here that you'll find hotels, cinemas and cafés, which are all notably lacking in Ragusa Ibla.

A memorable part of the town is the stately Baroque cathedral, **San Giovanni**, established in 1694. It is a very large building and has a fine terrace beyond its decorated western façade.

Another place to visit is the **Museo Archeologico** (open every morning and afternoon). It comprises a rather dusty collection of archaeological remains from various sites in the province. Among these are a **kiln** from Scornavacche (a former Greek colony known for pottery), finds from the **necropolis** at Camarina and some intricate **mosaics**.

The earthquake in 1693 split the town in two, revealing ruins and signs of early civilization. Business and industry thrives in Ragusa's upper town.

LA STRADA DEL VINO

Ragusa's Wine Route runs through the northwestern part of the province and takes in three of Sicily's best-known wineries: the **Donnafugata** wines (which actually grow around Vittorio), the much appreciated **Cerasuolo**, which are produced around Vittorio, and the **Ambrata** from Comiso. The area also supports sweet dessert wines, similar to marsala, produced on the coast in Trapani province. By prior appointment, a number of wineries are open to visitors who may wish to sample these and other local wines. Information is available at the tourist office in Ragusa: via Capitano Bocchieri 33, tel: 0932 622288 or 0932 621421.

FURTHER AFIELD FROM RAGUSA

The countryside around Ragusa has a number of interesting places to visit. The **Iblei Mountains** (*see* panel on page 81) are cultivated with orange trees, while the land and the south-flowing rivers slope to the sea from Ragusa. It is predominantly an agricultural area, which has scarcely been touched by tourism. Dry stone rubble walls weave over the topography keeping livestock in check and, on the coast, extensive cultivation under endless rows of greenhouses mars the scenery.

The Coastal Route ★

Marina di Ragusa is a typical seaside town, which comes to life during the summer months. Although intrinsically pretty, the coast beyond is blemished by too many plastic greenhouses – but there are a number of pleasant beaches and bathing areas, such as **Plaja Grande** and **Cava d'Aliga** between Camarina and Marina de Modica.

Donnafugata

Giuseppe Tomasi di Lampedusa took the name of this palace to describe another palace in *The Leopard*, but the building is quite different. It has recently been renovated and the palace and gardens of Donnafugata are a pleasant interlude. The gardens possess, amongst other interesting features, a fascinating **maze** and **grotto**. The palace itself is relatively modern; the 19th-century renovation of a 17th-century castle owes more to Venetian architecture than to Sicilian.

The area of Donnafugata, determined by the DOC (*Denominazione d'Origine Controllata*) label (*see* page 29), is also known for the production of some of Sicily's better wines, which are actually grown around the interesting Baroque town of Vittoria.

VISITING VITTORIA

Apart from being the capital of Ragusa province's wine production, Vittoria is also known for its elegant **Baroque buildings**. It is named after **Countess Vittoria Colonna**, who founded the town in 1607. The most gracious buildings are the **Madonna della Grazie**, rebuilt in 1754, and the neoclassical **Teatro Communale** beside it. The cathedral of **San Giovanni Battista**, reconstructed at the beginning of the 18th century after the 1693 earthquake, is also worth looking at. It has a hint of Africa in its architecture. There is a **Saturday morning market**, which is also pleasant to visit.

Modica **

Modica is located approximately 15km (almost 10 miles) from Ragusa and it is known for its fine Baroque buildings. This town is divided into two distinct zones: **Modica Bassa** (Lower Modica), through which Corso Umberto I runs, and **Modica Alta** (Upper Modica). Both zones hold fine buildings from the Spanish era.

The cathedral of **San Giorgio** marks the skyline of the upper part of town. It rises, in the best Sicilian tradition, above a grandiose flight of steps. It has five doors along the western front and is believed to be the 18th-century work of **Rosario Gagliardi**, who is also responsible for some of the better buildings in Noto (*see* page 92).

Modica Bassa is home to the town's second cathedral, **San Pietro**, which is also set above a flourish of Baroque stairs. Next door to this is the ex-convent of the Jesuits, which is another work by Gagliardi. The **Chiesa del Carmine**'s origins date back to the 15th-century Carmelite convent. The slightly more distant church of **Santa Maria del Gesù** illustrates the fine Gothic heritage left by the Spanish Catalan families who owned part of this area between the late 15th and mid-18th centuries.

Scicli *

This small town, which is slightly out of the way, abounds in fine Baroque buildings. It is here where the **Siculi**, who inhabited eastern Sicily, found their name. There is little evidence that suggests that this was once a prosperous Norman town, except for the outline of a ruined castle on the hilltop. If you are driving between the coast and Ragusa, stop a while and admire the 18th-century **Duomo** and the **Palazzo Fava** opposite it. The church of **San Giovanni** is worthwhile visiting for its oval interior and beautiful stucco work. The unusual Baroque façade of **Palazzo Beneventano** should also be observed.

> **COUNTRY TRADITIONS ON DISPLAY**
>
> Lovers of the popular arts should visit Modica's **Museo Ibleo delle Arti e Tradizioni Popolari** (Palazzo dei Mercedari, Via Mercè, open mornings and late afternoons) for an insight into rural life of the past. Country furniture, Sicilian carts, household furnishings and artisans' implements (arranged into the appropriate workshops) are all on display here.

Opposite: *Wines, candies and marzipan – a unique Sicilian selection.*
Below: *In true Baroque style, steps sweep up to Ragusa Ibla's cathedral.*

Southeast Sicily at a Glance

BEST TIMES TO VISIT

Because the area is slightly elevated, it is slightly cooler during the long, hot **summer** months. Siracusa has a fine, mild climate all year round and the cool, sunny days of **winter** are a good time to explore. **Spring** and **autumn** are noted for their wonderful display of natural colours.

GETTING THERE

The nearest **international airport** is at Catania (**Fontanarossa Airport**, tel: 095 349837 or 341654), located just 4km (2.5 miles) south of Catania. Catania itself is only 60km (37 miles) from Siracusa and 104km (65 miles) from Ragusa. Palermo is considerably further afield although there are three daily buses that travel from here to Siracusa. Both international airports receive scheduled and chartered flights. If you are in and around Noto or Ragusa, head for Siracusa and take the local bus transport. Siracusa, Noto, Modica and Ragusa are all on the Catania railway line. Connections are slow, but there are some attractive parts on the route. For all railway information, given in Italian, tel: 1478 88088, or website (also in English): www.fs-on-line.com.

GETTING AROUND

A car is almost essential in order to visit the smaller towns in the area. It is pos-

sible to travel by public transport, but your schedule should be flexible. There are excellent bus services oper-ated by SAIS and AST (in Siracusa, tel: 0931 462711) between Siracusa and Noto (40min), and adequate ones to Modica (2hr and 30min) and Ragusa (2hr and 50min). Frequent bus services to Catania (1hr and 15min) and Catania airport (1hr), leave from Siracusa. Contact Interbus-Etna, Siracusa, tel: 0931 66710. Serves Noto too. There is also a railway which has limited use for exploring this area.

WHERE TO STAY

LUXURY

Grand Hotel, viale Mazzini 12, Siracusa, tel: 0931 464600, fax: 0931 464611. Stylish palace hotel in prime area. Excellent restaurant.
Eremo della Giubiliana, contrada Giubiliana, Ragusa, tel: 0932 669119, fax: 0932 623891. A small, luxury hotel in converted convent, 9km (5.6 miles) south of town, with excellent restaurant.
Mediterraneo Palace, via Roma 189, Ragusa, tel: 0932 621944, fax: 0932 623799, e-mail: info@ mediterraneopalace.it Fine, modern hotel, in heart of town.

MID-RANGE

Domus Mariae, via Vittorio Veneto 76, Siracusa, tel: 0931

24854, fax: 0931 24858. At upper end of mid-range. A delightful, small hotel in a converted convent. On east-ern side of Ortygia.
Gran Bretagna, via Savoia 21, Siracusa, tel: 0931 68765, fax: 0931 462169. Great location. Good restaurant in pleasant hotel.
Villa Mediterranea, viale Lido, Marina di Noto, tel/fax: 0931 881840. Car necessary. Small hotel in pleasant garden setting.
Al Canisello, via Pavese 1, Noto, tel: 0931 835793, fax: 0931 837570, e-mail: canisello@tin.it Just 3km (2 miles) west of Via Roma. An old, renovated farm with private rooms. Small and very attractive, yet own car is needed.
Montreal, via San Guiseppe 8 (corner corso Italia), tel: 0932 621133, fax: 0932 621026. Modern hotel in the centre of Upper Ragusa with inexpensive restaurant.
Bristol, via Risorgimento 8/b, Modica, tel: 0932 762890, fax: 0932 763330. Not in the centre, but a good, comfort-able hotel. Car advised.

BUDGET

Hotel Aretusa, via F Crispi 75, Siracusa, tel/fax: 0931 24211. Near railway station. In modern part of town. Inexpensive, but pleasant rooms. Other budget hotels are in the neighbourhood.
Ambra, via Francesco

Southeast Sicily at a Glance

Giantommaso 14, Noto, tel: 0931 835554 or tel: 0330 795119, e-mail: currenti@polosud.it. Car necessary. Small, family hotel, bed and breakfast in large house.
San Giovanni, via Traspontino 3, Ragusa Superiore, tel: 0932 621013, . Overlooking the old pedestrian-only bridge. A bit dated, but good value.
Hotel Modica, Corso Umberto I, Modica, tel: 0932 941022, fax: 0932 941077. On the main street. A good, modern hotel.

LUXURY
Grand Hotel, *See Where to Stay.*
Arlecchino, Lungomare di Levante, tel: 0931 66386, Siracusa. A small seafood restaurant on the eastern shore of Ortygia with unusual decor. Less expensive pizzeria next door.

MID-RANGE
Trattoria Archimede, via Gemellaco 8, Siracusa, tel: 0931 69701. Established restaurant with broad seafood menu. Very popular.
Ristorante Duomo, via Cap. Bocchieri 31, Ragusa Ibla, tel: 0932 651265. Imaginative and innovative cuisine in a beautiful old palace.
Neas, Le Ristorante, via Rocco Pirri 30, Noto, tel: 0931 573538. In a former palace.

Comfortable with good, local fare. Inexpensive for category.
La Pergola, piazza Luigi Sturzo 6, Ragusa Superiore, tel: 0932 255659. Difficult to find (it is northwest of Ecce Homo church), but well worth the effort for its fine cuisine.
Fattoria delle Torri, vico Napolitano 14, Modica, tel: 0932 751286. Near Piazza Matteoti. Renowned for its authentic Sicilian cuisine.
Opera, via Carlo Alberto 133/b, Vittoria, tel: 0932 869129. A fine restaurant with seafood specialities.

BUDGET
Trattoria La Foglia, via Capodieci 29, Siracusa, tel: 0931 66233. Small, attractive trattoria. Specializing in inexpensive vegetarian and Mediterranean cuisine.
Spaghetteria do Scogghiu, via Scina 11, Siracusa (no phone). A large and popular venue. Homely food and great value for money.
Al Ficodindia, via C M Arezzo 7-9, Siracusa, tel: 0931 462838. True home cooking and very popular.
Il Barocco, via Cavour, Noto,

tel: 0951 835999. Local specialities at inexpensive prices.
Trattoria La Rusticana, via XXV Aprile, Ragusa Ibla, tel: 0932 227981. Very popular. Good cuisine and fine pastas.

This is an area of traditional skills and intensive agriculture. Siracusa is known (as are many other towns) for its marzipan confections. Antica Drogheria (corso XXV Aprile 59/61, Ragusa Ibla, tel: 0932 652090) is a good address for fine cheeses, wines and Sicilian specialities.

Ufficio di Turismo, via San Sebastiano 45, tel: 0931 67710, Siracusa, and via Maestranza 33, Siracusa, tel: 0931 464255 or 481200
Ufficio di Turismo, Piazza XVI Maggio, Noto, tel: 0931 836744.
Ufficio di Turismo, via Capitano Bocchieri 33, Ragusa Ibla, tel: 0932 622288 or 621421.
Ufficio di Turismo, corso Umberto I 296, Modica, tel: 0932 752747.

SIRACUSA	J	F	M	A	M	J	J	A	S	O	N	D
AVERAGE TEMP. °F	50	51	54	58	65	73	79	80	75	67	59	53
AVERAGE TEMP. °C	10	11	12	14	18	23	26	27	24	19	15	12
HOURS OF SUN DAILY	3	3	5	7	8	10	10	9	8	6	4	3
RAINFALL in	3	1.9	1.6	1.5	0.9	0.4	0.2	0.6	1.4	3.9	2.2	3.4
RAINFALL mm	76	48	41	38	23	10	5	15	35	99	56	86
DAYS OF RAINFALL	9	8	5	5	2	1	2	1	6	8	10	9

6
Eastern Sicily

The active, and sometimes menacing, volcano of **Mount Etna** dominates this part of Sicily. It has fashioned the landscape and been responsible for the destruction (notably in 1669) of settlements along this attractive coast. Yet the snow-capped peak is beautiful and many visitors climb the mountain through the **Parco Nazionale dell'Etna** to gain better insight into this powerful natural phenomenon.

The main city on this eastern coast is **Catania**. The port and industrial centre form the second-largest city in Sicily. Northwards along the shoreline, with the ever-present reminder of Mount Etna to the west, the road winds through the smart Baroque town of **Acireale** and further towards the popular towns of **Giardini-Naxos** (noted for its fine beach hotels) and **Naxos** (the first Greek settlement in Sicily). **Taormina**, one of the island's most photogenic towns, leans against the lower slopes of Mount Etna and faces the open Ionian Sea.

The 5km (3-mile) **Strait of Messina** separates the northeastern tip of Sicily from the toe of Italy. Linked by frequent ferries to the mainland and offering onward shipping services to the volcanic **Aeolian Islands**, Messina has grown because of its maritime connections. It was also the birthplace of Antonello da Messina, one of the few successful Sicilian artists in Renaissance Italy.

The hot springs of the Aeolian Islands prove very therapeutic for invalids who flock here each year. The Aeolian Islands prospered with the manufacture of **obsidian** – a black volcanic glass.

Mare Tirreno (Tyrrhenian Sea)

I. di Ustica   Isola Eolie

Palermo   Messina
                Taormina
Isola   Mare Ionio
Egadi   Catania   (Ionian
                    Sea)
I. di Pantelleria

Mare Mediterraneo
(Mediterranian Sea)

DON'T MISS

*** **Taormina:** for its fine Greek theatre.
*** **Mount Etna:** experience this sight close up.
*** **Stromboli:** for its volcanic activity.
** **Aeolian Islands:** go on a cruise or stay in these isles.
** **Museo Archeologico, Lipari:** one of Sicily's greatest archaeological collections.
* **Museo Regionale di Messina:** a fine collection of sculpture and paintings.

Opposite: *According to legend, the rocks of Aci Trezza were hurled at the fleeing Ulysses by the blinded Cyclops.*

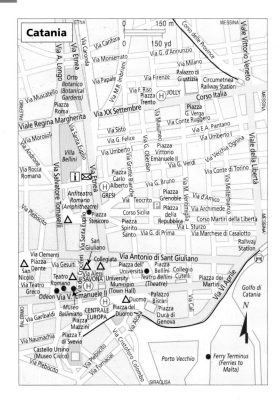

CATANIA

There are few ancient remains from the Greek colony of 2700 years ago who once lived in the area. Earthquakes wiped out much of the town in both 1169 and 1693, and the large flow of lava that followed the cataclysmic 1669 eruption swallowed further areas.

Modern Catania is centred on Via Etnea, an elegant axis where the city's elite shop around the beautiful **Piazza del Duomo** in the shadow of Mount Etna.

Piazza del Duomo **

The site of an active and interesting fish market in the mornings, the elegant Piazza del Duomo is beautifully illuminated in the evenings. Note the unusual **fountain** in its centre: a lava elephant carrying an Egyptian obelisk on its back.

The Duomo, the town's Baroque cathedral, was originally built in the 11th century and dedicated to the town's patron saint, Agata. It has been rebuilt various times, but its magnificent **Baroque façade** (by Vaccarini) has withstood the last three centuries. Remains of the Norman building have been discovered inside and they can be viewed under the nave. The cathedral houses the tomb (by Giovanni Battista Tassara) of Catania's **Vincenzo Bellini** (1801–35), whose operas, *Norma* and *La Sonnambula*, are internationally renowned.

Other tombs include the beautiful sepulchre of Queen Constance of Aragon (wife of Frederick III) in the

---

SAN NICOLÒ

Not to be missed is the Benedictine church of San Nicolò and the beautiful monastery adjacent to it. This complex dates back to the 16th century, although much of it was completed in the 18th century. It is richly decorated (some would say too richly for a religious order) and recalls the decoration of **Palazzo Biscari**, near the Duomo.

Cappella della Madonna, where the ashes of her husband, and other nobles, fill an ancient sarcophagus. Giovanni Battista Mazzola was responsible for the doorway to this chapel and his son, Gian Domenico Mazzola, created the northern doorway and arch leading into the Norman **Cappella del Crocifisso**.

Vaccarini added the finishing details to the *municipio* (the town hall), which is adjacent to the cathedral and on the other side of the busy Via Vittorio Emanuele II. View the intricate façade of **Palazzo Biscari**, which was once the home of the 18th-century Prince of Biscari (whose private collection is now exhibited in the Museo Civico, *see* panel, this page).

The beautiful, classical façade of **Teatro Massimo Bellini** is illuminated at night and its fine architecture is apparent. The theatre was inaugurated with a performance of Bellini's *Norma* in 1890.

Castello Ursino **

A walk southwest through the columned **Piazza Mazzini** (the columns were used in a previous Roman basilica) will take you to the Norman silhouette of Castello Ursino on **Piazza Federico di Svevia**. It was originally built (for Frederick II) on the seaboard, but the 1669 lava flows pushed the shore seaward and surrounded the building with a lava pavement. It was restored in 1837 and it now houses the Museo Civico.

Via dei Crociferi **

Built in the 18th century, this street is lined with elegant city palaces, wealthy homes, Baroque churches and convents. You will find the birthplaces of both Giovanni Verga (**Museo Verga**, open mornings and late afternoons on Tuesdays, Thursdays and Fridays) and Vincenzo Bellini (**Museo Belliniano**, open

---

ORTO BOTANICO (BOTANICAL GARDENS)

North of Villa Bellini lies the pleasant public garden of Orto Botanico (open weekday mornings). It is a refreshing place to stroll and observe the many plants and trees that grow on this island. This botanical garden is renowned for its collection of **cacti**.

MUSEO CIVICO

The **Castello Ursino** now houses the Museo Civico (open mornings only), which was restored in 1837. This museum holds an amalgamated collection of **Roman artefacts**, medieval pieces, **Renaissance paintings** and later sculpture. Amongst these exhibits look out for some superb icons, retables, and paintings by **Ribera** and the school of **Caravaggio**.

Below: *Castello Ursino, now housing the Museo Civico in Catania.*

SANT'AGATA

Two churches that are dedicated to Saint Agatha (the patron saint of Catania), **Sant'Agata al Carcere** and **Sant'Agata alla Fornace** (also called San Biagio), are situated along Via Etnea. The former marks the spot where the saint was imprisoned in the 3rd century and the latter was built on the site where Saint Agatha was burned to death (hence the church's name).

mornings only). The latter is near the sparse remains of the **Foro Romano**, and the once imposing **Teatro Romano**, dating from the 5th century BC. The street ends in the **Palazzo Cerami**, now part of the university.

Via Etnea *

Stretching for nearly 3km (over 1.5 miles) from the town hall (on the northern side of the cathedral) to the lower slopes of Mount Etna, Via Etnea has the unusual distinction of being paved with **lava slabs**. The lower part of the road is largely free of cars, which makes strolling through the smart fashion shops, bookstores and sidewalk cafés a hassle-free pleasure. When the 15th-century university buildings were rebuilt after the 1693 earthquake, it was Vaccarini who designed **Palazzo Sanguiliano** and laid out the **Piazza dell'Università**.

Piazza Stesicoro, built on top of a Roman amphitheatre, is the city's modern centre. The dark remains of this ancient monument lie incongruously in the centre. Further north is the delightful **Villa Bellini**, which is a late 19th-century public garden with a bust depicting this city's famous son.

Below: *Villa Bellini's gardens provide a pleasant place for relaxing in central Catania.*

AROUND CATANIA

The northbound coastal road from Catania, gradually leaves the rather uninspiring city suburbs and, with Mount Etna on its left, leads through heavily-perfumed orange and lemon groves to **Aci Castello**. This small town is well known for both its castle (open in the mornings and late afternoons), located on a promontory, and its attractive little port filled with brightly painted fishing boats.

Faraglioni dei Ciclopi *
The legend of Cyclops **Polyphemus**, who is blind in his only eye, tells of how he hurled these lava rocks at his aggressor, **Ulysses**, and now, lying in the shallows, they form an extraordinary sight off the coast at **Aci Trezza**.

Part of what is known as the **Cyclops Riviera**, the charming little town of Aci Trezza hugs the coast and a colourful fishing fleet populates the harbour. The restaurants and *trattorie* along the waterfront have a good reputation for fish. Note all the crunchy bits underfoot – they are fragments of airborne debris from Mount Etna.

Above: *Aci Trezza is known for its excellent seafood restaurants.*

Acireale ***
This area is acclaimed for its **lemons**, sulphurous **thermal waters**, *pupi* **puppet theatre**, annual **carnival**, and *cassata siciliana* ice cream. Acireale has a stately Baroque face (all was rebuilt in the early 18th century).

The heart of the town is the **Piazza del Duomo**, formerly known as the Piazza del Cinque d'Oro, named after a card game. It is dominated by the lovely Baroque **Basilica de Santi Pietro e Paolo** (dating from 1608) and the Duomo (established in the 16th century – the pseudo-Gothic façade was added later). The two **bell towers** were constructed in the 20th century according to plans drawn up by the eminent architect, Giovanni Battista Basile. On the same piazza lies the handsome Baroque **Palazzo Comunale** (the town hall). The Corso Umberto I, running north of the piazza, is a fine street with very good shops, solid palaces and a multitude of open-air cafés. Book lovers should visit the **Biblioteca Zelantea** and its **Pinacoteca** (open in the mornings on Mondays and Wednesdays) where its collection of over 100,000 volumes constitutes the most substantial book assortment in Sicily.

WATER THERAPY

Acireale's thermal waters have been used therapeutically for over 2000 years, due to their sulphurous and radioactive properties. Today, they attract Italians seeking relief for **dermatological**, **respiratory** and **gynaecological** conditions, **arthritis** and problems relating to the ears, nose and throat. Although the 1873 neo-classical **Santa Venera Spa** still enjoys a fine reputation, the smart new **Santa Caterina Spa**, overlooking the sea, has more modern facilities. Here, mud and sulphurous waters are used therapeutically in tandem with physiotherapy and bathing in the heated pool.

Right: *An early-morning view of Mount Etna.*
Opposite: *A profusion of plants grows on the fertile slopes of Mount Etna.*

MOUNT ETNA POINTERS

Mount Etna is a violent and active volcano and there are risks involved if climbing to its summit, so all official advice must be heeded. It rises to over 3300m (10,000ft) and will often be bitterly cold at the summit (with temperatures below zero), even in summer. There is no access to the summit in winter. Take warm clothing or rent this from the **Rifugio Sapienza**, which also has a restaurant and a hostel. The Refuge also organizes an excursion to the top, taking visitors in small groups. Before leaving on an independent trip, call SITAS in Nicolosi on tel: 095 911158 or 095 914209 for up-to-date climatic and seismic data. The best views from and of Mount Etna are the privilege of early risers. Those who see Etna at **dawn** are often rewarded with spectacular panoramas. Later in the day the peak is covered with clouds and the views are lost. Lastly, a private railway (**Ferrovia Circumetnea**, tel: 095 541250 for information) follows a route around the mountain. It leaves Catania and travels in a clockwise direction Via Adrano, Bronte, Linguaglossa and Giarre-Riposto, where you can connect with a local line or a bus back to Catania.

Mount Etna

Snow-capped Mount Etna peaks at 3323m (10,900ft) and is one of the most active and dangerous volcanoes in the world. Over 30 serious eruptions have taken place over the last two centuries, whilst the most devastating in modern history took place in 1669. The villages and towns that surround the lower levels are under a constant threat. Over the past century a number of people have lost their lives along the crater rims, yet the real estate on the mountain slopes is appealing to the brave and curious. Because of the volcano's nigh-unpredictable nature, routes to the summit are constantly subject to change or even closure.

Sicily's only ski resort, **Piano Provenzana**, lies on the flanks of this seething cauldron. It is located on the northern slopes of the mountain and it offers five ski lifts and a **skiing season** of several weeks (depending on the mountain's eruptions).

In 1987 some 50,000ha (123,500 acres) of the mountain and its foothills were declared a national park, known as **Parco Nazionale dell'Etna**, in order to protect its unique flora and to prevent the ever-encroaching development on its eastern flanks.

The ascent of Mount Etna can be made from both the north and south sides and it is possible to get to the top of Mount Etna and back from Catania in a day. The town of **Nicolosi**, some 10km (6 miles) from Catania, is the position of access from the south side of the mountain. It is also the way to the **Rifugio Sapienza**, which is the starting point for guided visits – using the cableway, bus or shank's pony – to reach the last 100m (approximately 110yd) above the Torre del Filosofo and journey to a point near the central crater. At the summit lie the three great craters known as the **central crater**, the **northeast crater** and the **southeast crater**. Each of these has brought destruction to the eastern part of Sicily.

Among the most spectacular sights on Mount Etna is the **Valle del Bove**. It is a vast gash near the southeast crater, nearly 20km (12 miles) in circumference, with three sides of lava walls rising to a height of over 900m (2953ft). It is covered with scores of small craters and smouldering fumeroles and it is here that many of the eruptions during the mid-20th century took place.

If one is staying in the Taormina, Naxos or Messina areas, the most convenient way to access the peak of Mount Etna is from the north side (Via **Linguaglossa**) and the winter ski resort of Piano Provenzana. This route passes the new **Observatory** (the old one was destroyed in the 1971 eruption). This area has been devoid of volcanic activity for approximately three decades and the route takes you through beautiful pine forests and up to still-smoking lava fields.

The Vegetation

Because of the fertile quality of the volcanic soil, the area around Mount Etna supports rich vegetation. Citrus groves abound amongst the recently planted walnuts, cherries, pistachios, almonds and vineyards. Deciduous oak forests, chestnuts and beeches interspersed with brilliant broom characterize the higher slopes, giving way, at a greater altitude, to the vast pine forests.

> **ACI CASTELLO AND HER SISTER TOWNS**
>
> The son of Pan, **Acis**, was a shepherd near the slopes of Mount Etna, but met his death at the hands of the Cyclops, **Polyphemus**, who was **Ulysses'** nemesis. They both loved the beautiful **Galatea**, but she only loved Acis. One legend relates that Polyphemus cut Acis into nine pieces and on the site of each of these arose a settlement with the name Aci. Another legend relates that, with help from **Zeus**, Galatea transformed her body into the River Akis and as she cried out the name of her beloved, the wind carried the sound to the nine villages, which now bear the names Aci: Acireale, Aci Castello, Aci Trezza, Aci Catena, Aci San Filippo, Aci Bonacorsi, Aci Platani, Aci San Antonio, and Aci Santa Lucia.

ORNITHOLOGICAL FRIVOLITY

Near Taormina's Greek Theatre is the **Parco Duca di Cesarò** (also known as **Giardino Trevelyan**). This is a fine garden that was once owned by British amateur ornithologist, **Lady Florence Trevelyan**. Amid the blooms are some extraordinary ornithological follies and a series of unusual bird boxes and hides from which Lady Trevelyan was able to observe her feathered visitors. This garden is now open to the public.

TAORMINA AND THE COAST

Exiled residents of Naxos founded **Tauromenium** in 403BC. Taormina, as it is now known, has through the millennia, been visited and fêted by many a prominent traveller. Once allied with Rome, then the capital of Byzantine Sicily, Taormina was destroyed and rebuilt by the Arabs. Remnants exist from each of its political eras.

Since Taormina is definitely the resort for Sicilians and on every tourist's must list, it is often **very crowded**. Its patrician palaces, **stunning views**, gardens bursting with subtropical flowers, and expensive **restaurants** and **cafés** attract the elite. Although it is easily reachable on a day trip from Catania, it merits a stay of its own. Please note that the centre is off limits to cars, so use the car parks and walk, or take the cableway from the car park at Mazzarò.

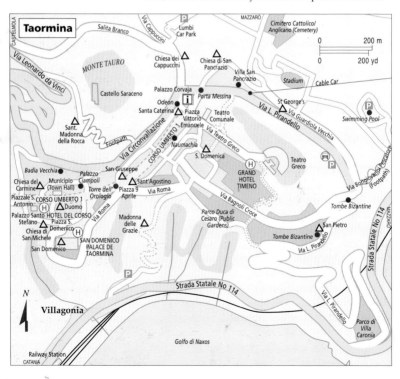

Teatro Greco ★★★

A superb site between Mount Etna and the Ionian Sea sets the scene for this theatre (open every day until dusk), which was originally built by the **Greeks** and modified by the **Romans**. It is second in size to the theatre at Siracusa and, with its **near-perfect acoustics**, provides an ideal venue for the annual summer arts festival (from the mid-July to September).

Above: *A magnificent setting for Taormina's Graeco-Roman theatre.*

Central Taormina ★★

The **Corso Umberto I**, the pulse of Taormina, winds its way downhill from the **Porta Messina** to the Duomo. It is closed in parts to vehicular traffic and is the thoroughfare for well-heeled shoppers and people watchers. One can occasionally glimpse the Ionian Sea. Small side streets drop away from the main road and there are old routes where traditions still endure. **Piazza Vittorio Emanuele** is where you'll find the tourist office housed in part of the Palazzo Corvaja, a beautiful palace dating back to the 13th century, which now also houses the **Museo Siciliano di Artee Tradizioni Popolari** (well worth a visit). Halfway down is the **Piazzale 9 Aprile**, which is surrounded by buildings on three sides and opens to views over the Ionian Sea. The city gate, **Torre dell'Orologio**, is also a spectacular sight.

On the way to the 13th-century Duomo, dedicated to **San Nicolò**, you pass the *municipio* and the **Palazzo Ciampoli** – both have interesting façades. The *ex-convento* **San Domenico** is a luxury hotel with gardens.

Palazzo Santo Stefano and Palazzo Ciampoli ★★

One of the last places to have been held by the Normans, **Palazzo Santo Stefano** and its beautiful surrounding gardens is another Norman gem. It was built for the dukes of Santo Stefano in the 15th century and it

> **WHO WAS WHO IN SICILY'S PAST**
>
> **Barbarian** – anyone the Greeks considered non-Greek.
> **Carthaginians** – earlier called Phoenicians.
> **Dorians** – came from an area that comprises Rhodes, the Pelaponnese and Crete.
> **Elymians** – a tribe of early Mediterranean origin.
> **Ionians** – Greeks from the area between Greece and Asia Minor.
> **Phoenicians** – *see* above.
> **Saracens** – Arabs, Berbers and Spanish Moors.
> **Sicani** – tribes inhabiting western Sicily, possibly originally from Libya, Syria or the Iberia Peninsula.
> **Siculi** – tribes inhabiting eastern Sicily, having invaded from mainland Italy.

Above: *Aptly named Beautiful Island, Isola Bella lies just below Taormina.*

harks back to previous Gothic and Norman styles. Take a look at the unusual lozenge-shaped frieze done in black lava and white stone. Surrounded by a pleasant, small garden, the palace houses a permanent exhibition of sculpture. Once an extraordinary palace, though largely ruined by rude architectural changes in the 20th century, **Palazzo Ciampoli** still manages to diffuse some of its original splendour.

The Beaches *

Tides around **Isola Bella** have created twin sandy beaches that link the shore to the islet. The best beaches (though very crowded in season and not always well maintained) are north of **Mazzarò** at **Spisone** and **Mazzeo**. Near **Capo San Alessio**, 10km (6 miles) to the north, there are better and less crowded beaches.

Naxos **

It was on the lava form of Capo Schisò, some 8km (5 miles) south of Taormina, where the first Greeks arrived in 734BC and established a settlement in Sicily. They named it Naxos, after one of the Cyclades Islands, and within five years other settlements were beginning to establish themselves on this stretch of coast.

The excavations and exhibits in the **Museo Archeologico** (open daily) are interesting tourist attractions. The town survived various changes of rule until Dionysius I destroyed it in 405BC. Parts of the old city walls, as well as the west gate, still remain. Have a look at the two **kilns**; one is used for firing *pithoi* (for which Naxos was renowned) and vases, and the other for firing tiles. There are also remains of a simple **temple** and a

---

THE VERSATILE CITRUS

Moro, *Tarocco* and *Sanguinello* are all types of *sanguine* (blood) oranges. They burst with juice and may be dark or light red in colour. *Feminello* and *Verdello* are Sicily's favourite species of lemons. These all grow in Sicily and particularly on Mount Etna's fertile slopes. Apart from drinking or eating citrus, essential oils for **perfumes** and flavouring are extracted (from lemons in particular). The **peel** is candied and pectin is made from the peel and pips. Oil molasses is created and a range of **aromas** for the food industry are extracted.

7th-century *tememos* (a sacred enclosure dedicated to Aphrodite). The setting of these ruins is a delight, yet it is limited. Fruit and flowering trees abound in this area and this is a refreshing contrast to the modern town that is now known as Giardini-Naxos.

The museum houses items which predate the Greeks as well as other antiquities. Among the Greek exhibits are a 7th-century BC marble lamp, items from the 8th-6th century BC **necropolis**, scores of *pithoi*, various vases and votive jars, dozens of **antefixes** and the moulds in which they were made, bronze helmets, anchors and a charming statue of Aphrodite on horseback.

Giardini-Naxos *

The 'Gardens of Naxos', once a small fishing hamlet, are better known for the numerous small hotels and restaurants that have sprouted along the shoreline offering sun starved northerners the chance of sun and sea. The pleasant town has a narrow beach and it provides a convenient base from which to explore Taormina and, indeed, Mount Etna.

Gole Alcàntara *

The Alcàntara Gorge was formed from lava by the fast-flowing river, which shaped a narrow gorge over the millennia. Named **Al Qantarah** by the Saracens, the river and its gorge have become a popular tourist spot. **Tours** exploring the gorge are organized in the drier summer months (galoshes and waders are provided) and one can wade upstream for some 200m (220yd). At places the sheer walls of the gorge obstruct the sky and one cannot help but be awed by Nature's unstoppable force. It can become perilous inside the gorge, with the freezing cold waterfalls and many types of biting insects proving to be obstacles.

> **ANTEFIXES**
>
> Those little terracotta sculptures, the size of a small saucer and bearing cross faces, are antefixes. They were produced by the Greeks to mask the unaesthetic gap between the tiled roof and cornice. There is an excellent collection of these items at the Museo Archeologico at **Naxos** and also in **Lipari**'s fine Museo Archeologico.

Below: *A collection of small Greek antefixes on display in the Museo Archeologico at Naxos. The classical town was known for its pottery and in particular for these ugly little faces.*

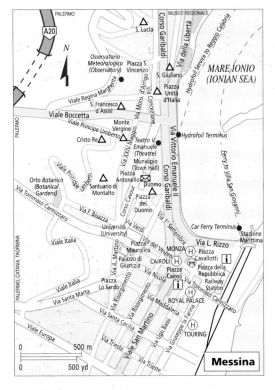

MESSINA

There is a busy port at the northeastern tip of Sicily and this is the point of departure for a short ferry ride across the 5km (2-mile) Messina Strait to mainland Reggio di Calabria. Despite its old Greek origins, it is now a modern city since it was largely rebuilt after the catastrophic earthquake nearly a century ago and again after the World War II bombardment. It now ranks as the third-largest town in Sicily.

Piazza del Duomo **

Piazza del Duomo is the pulse of old Messina and is situated just beyond the harbour. Its present form is the result of 18th-century city planning and

it is largely free of traffic. The centrepiece of the piazza is the pretty **Fontana di Orione**, a 16th-century fountain depicting four rivers, crafted by Tuscan Montorsoli.

Duomo *

This cathedral may appear to be Norman, but on closer inspection it is evident that is a modern reconstruction. It was rebuilt after the 1908 earthquake and subsequently after the World War II bombing, incorporating the few original elements that where still intact. Despite its recent construction it is a faithful replica of the earlier cathedral. Its fabulous **treasury** (open every afternoon, except Mondays) is exceptionally well displayed and houses some interesting religious artefacts including a

Left: *A panoramic view of Messina with Reggio di Calabria in the background.* **Opposite:** *The beautiful fountain of Orion, sculpted by Montorsoli.*

number of delicately wrought silver items (Messina was renowned for its silversmiths), such as the 12th-century reliquary of the arm of San Maziano and the various interesting reliquaries and items concerning the **Madonna della Lettera**.

Beside the cathedral stands the belfry with its 20th-century *orologio astronomico* (a huge astronomical clock reputed to be the largest in the world). It was built in 1933 by a Strasbourg firm and on the chimes of midday there is a 10-minute performance by its many mechanical parts to the strains of Schubert's *Ave Maria*.

Santissima Annunziata dei Catalani **

This university chapel was once a Norman church (open only during services) and its glorious **exterior** is worth a detour. The church was originally constructed by Catalan merchants, and its delicate arcades and a fine cupola all date back to the 12th century.

Museo Regionale **

This museum (Via della Libertà, open every morning and in the summer afternoons on Tuesdays, Thursdays and Saturdays) is the highlight of any visit to Messina. It displays items dating from Byzantine and Norman times to the 18th century. Among the most interesting pieces is the polyptych of the *Madonna with St Gregory and St Benedict* by **Antonello da Messina**, as well as **Caravaggio**'s *Adoration of the Shepherds* and his very brooding *Resurrection of Lazarus*. The museum also offers sculptures by members of the **Gagini** family, sculptures

CARAVAGGIO

Born Michelangelo Merisi da Caravaggio (Caravaggio is a village near Bergamo) in 1571, he was distantly related to the Sforza, Colonna and Borromeo families. He was brought up in Milan, but travelled to Rome in 1592 where he became familiar with the artistic community. He was often in trouble and in 1605 he fled to **Genoa** after wounding a writer. In 1606 he was instrumental in the death of a young man during a violent ball game. He travelled to Malta, where he found refuge and patrons in the **Cavaliers of Malta**. Paralleling his life, his style became darker, more brooding and troubled. He got into trouble yet again in Malta and was imprisoned, but he managed to escape and sought refuge in **Messina**, Sicily. He lived there for a year, from 1608 to 1609, and then left for Naples where he was attacked unexpectedly in an inn. The pope finally pardoned him for his crimes, but on his journey back to Rome, in 1610, he died at **Porto Ercole** under very mysterious circumstances.

by **Francesco Laurana** (a master of many *Madonna and Child* sculptures), a delicately glazed blue and white *Mother and Child* medallion in terracotta from the studio of the **della Robbia** family, and some bold paintings by Messina-born **Girolamo Alibrandi** (1470–1524).

Above: *On the neck of a vase in the Museo Archeologico, Lipari, is a unique design depicting the* Labours of Hercules.

Milazzo *

This town has developed around the **Cape of Milazzo**, which is a strip of land extending into the Tyrrhenian Sea, and it is easily accessed from Messina, just 41km (25 miles) away. Its origins date back to Greek times when it was an important port known as Mylae. Today it is the point of departure for the beautiful Aeolian Islands to the north of Sicily. It also has a charm of its own and its **seafront promenade**, the *lungomare*, is a pleasant place to take a stroll.

Before taking to the islands, set aside an hour or two to visit the bustling **morning fish market**, admire the **Carmine** and its former Carmelitani convent (restored 16th- and 18th-century buildings) and see the 13th-century **castle** (open mornings and afternoons, except on Mondays), which is built on the base of an existing Arab fortress by Frederick II.

AEOLIAN ISLANDS

This string of small, stark and solitary islands is hardly known beyond the country's borders, yet they are one of the most beautiful sights in Italy. **Tourism** (the islands are very crowded in summer) and **fishing** fill the coffers of the islanders who live in picturesque, small villages. With rapid hydrofoils and frequent ferry services it is possible to visit a couple of the islands within a day or, better still, to stay at one of the many hotels and take a night excursion by boat to see the natural **fireworks**

GREEK MASKS

Dating from the late 4th century BC, and onwards, a fine selection of some 250 Greek theatrical masks is on display in the **Archaeological Museum** in Lipari. They were made by the great artist **Menandro** (342–290BC) and almost all of them are identifiable thanks to the catalogue produced in Roman times, which lists the Greek characters. They are roughly divided into five main categories: old men, old women, handsome young men, slaves and beautiful young women. The museum also has a series of small statuettes, which portray the main characters of theatrical pieces.

from Stromboli. Cars are only permitted on Vulcano, Lipari, Salina and Filicudi (although it is more convenient to leave your car in one of the many garages in Milazzo and hire local transport).

Lipari **

The largest of the islands, Lipari, is a 60-minute trip by fast hydrofoil from Milazzo. It has a very pretty town of the same name and a couple of other smaller villages. In ancient times it was known for its reserves of **obsidian.** The two ports are exceptionally picturesque and therefore very crowded in summer.

There is a 27km (16-mile) tour of the island, which includes **Canneto**, **Aquacalda** and **Quatrocchi** and offers a great panorama of the archipelago.

Museo Archeologico ***

This museum keeps the islands' most important finds in its fortified castle and cathedral complex (open each morning and afternoon). It is truly outstanding and of great importance archaeologically. The different cultures that have inhabited the islands are informatively presented. The prehistory section, devoted to Lipari when the obsidian mining was of great value, is particularly interesting. Highlights of the museum include the fabulous hoard of 2nd- and 3rd-century BC **amphorae** (which were recovered from wrecks and are displayed in tiers), the reconstructed **burial sites**, some superb **kraters**, an unusual 4th-century BC

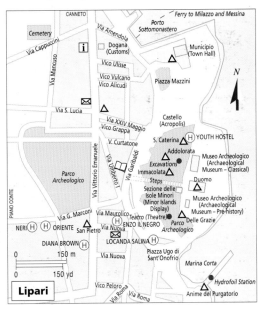

Lipari

VOLCANIC TERMINOLOGY

There are four types of volcanic eruptions of which two take their name from their Sicilian examples: Stromboli and Vulcano. Strombolian eruptions are moderate, fairly continuous, and the lava flows are followed by periods of inactivity. Vulcanic eruptions are far more liquid and explosive and they produce lava, gases, pyroclastic material (solids melted or regurgitated by the volcano), ash and pumice-like lava. The other two types of eruptions are Hawaiian and Plinian.

vase by Antimenes (with painted decorations of the battle of Hydra inside the neck of the vase) and scores of theatrical statues and votives.

Vulcano **

This island, still smouldering and puffing out sulphurous gases on its northeast side, was the site for the fiery forges of the Greek god of fire, **Vulcan**. It has three craters and is the island nearest to the coast. Although matters could change, it has been over a century since the last eruption and there are plenty of permanent settlers and some excellent hotels.

An intriguing highlight on a visit to this 21km² (14 square mile) island is the ascent to its crater: a two-hour, round-trip walk through fields of evil-smelling sulphurous gas. This is not for the sensitive.

Salina **

Salina is one of the prettiest of the seven islands. It is known for its extinct volcanoes, its **capers** and the sweet dessert wine, **malvasia**, so beloved by Caesar. The fertile land also supports beautiful deciduous forests, which are now protected as a **nature reserve**. The island is saddle-shaped and two volcanic peaks – one rising to the highest point of the Aeolian Islands at 962m (3300ft) –

Below: *The peak of Vulcano still smoulders above its calm waters.*

dominate a lower, fertile valley and over-shadow the charming main town of **Santa Marina Salina**. It is a town with two streets that run along the waterfront and it boasts delightful pastel-coloured buildings. **Scuba diving** and **fishing** trips are two of Salina's main attractions. To the west lies **Rinelli di Leni**, another small port.

Panarea ***

The 3.5km² (1.4 square mile) reef around Panarea has taken the lives of many a sailor and sunk his cargo. Today the reefs provide Italy with one of its favourite **snorkelling** and **scuba diving** destinations on what is the oldest, and possibly the loveliest, of the seven main islands. Volcanically heated waters surge near the harbour on what has become the exclusive hideaway of famous and wealthy northerners. The many cube-shaped homes, in dazzling white and pale pastels, attest to the development of the island.

Above: *One of the prettiest Aeolian Islands, Panarea is a popular retreat for wealthy northern Italians.*

The prehistoric village of **Punta Milazzese** also enjoyed an era of prosperity in the 2nd millennium BC. A walk to this point reveals vestiges of this once important settlement.

Stromboli ***

This is Italy's most active volcano. Trips to see the pyrotechnics are a must for anyone staying on the Aeolian Islands between May and October. A **night excursion** to this volcano, spewing fire and magma every 15 to 20 minutes, is mesmerizing. During the day, one can join a six-hour round trip **climb to the crater** atop the conical 924m (3080ft) mountain, and watch the impressive cauldron only metres away.

Stromboli has delightful **Arab-style houses**, fashioned like white sugar cubes, on the bleak and fascinating landscape. The island is also known for its sweet, golden wine known as **malvasia**.

MUD, GLORIOUS MUD

A popular Vulcano experi-ence are the **mud baths** located just off the beach and to the east of the har-bour. A 20-minute immersion in the sea (wear shoes as some of the underwater rocks are extremely hot) in the early morning or evening, followed by a shower (as the mud is radioactive), has proven therapeutic effects on **rheumatism** and **dermato-logical problems**.

Above: *Regular ferries and hydrofoils link the Aeolian Islands.*

Filicudi and Alicudi **

Filicudi and Alicudi are further afield and less frequented than the other islands, though both are worth a visit for their extreme beauty. Filicudi was inhabited in the Bronze Age (the prehistoric village on **Capo Graziano** can be visited), but today these islands have few residents (Alicudi has only 150 inhabitants). There are no roads or information offices here – it is just plain island wilderness.

THE NORTH COAST

This once slightly remote coast has become a favourite amongst holidaymakers and now the area boasts plenty of hotels, especially in Palermo province, around Cefalù. The north coast of Messina province was also an area in which the Greeks settled millennia ago, and parts of the coastal areas are very pretty. There are extensive olive groves and some citrus plantations. The intense agriculture is accentuated by the ever-present fragrance of wild herbs. If you are travelling on the *autostrada*, you'll find that the route takes you over limestone gorges, dry river beds and bridges, and through mountains, hills and a never-ending series of tunnels. The whole motorway is an exceptional model of Italian engineering.

Tindari *

The town of Tindari lies on the site of the former city of **Tyndaris**, a strategic Siracusan settlement founded over 2300 years ago. The somewhat over-run, but nevertheless interesting, ruins (open each day until dusk) are in a spectacular position, 280m (850ft) above the sea, and evoke images of the town founded by Dionysius the Elder, after his victorious defeat of the Carthaginians. The interesting features at this site include the largely rebuilt **theatre** with its typically Greek maritime back-

PATTI

Not far from the ruins of Tindari, in a hilly area where the Greeks and Romans once lived, lies the interesting medieval village of Patti. The cathedral is particularly interesting, for within its 14th-century walls are countless art treasures, including the marble sepulchre of **Adelaide** (Roger de Hauteville's wife and the mother of King Roger II). The landscape between Tindari and Patti is worth the journey alone. Amateur archaeologists might also like to visit the **Roman Villa** near Marina di Patti, which was discovered during the building of the motorway in the 1970s. It is not particularly well maintained, but does have some splendid mosaics.

drop (used under the Romans for gladiatorial fights), the beautifully constructed 3rd-century BC **basilica,** and various floor **mosaics**. Near the archaeological ruins is the massive **Sanctuary of the Black Madonna** (a venerated statue of the Virgin). Equally impressive are the views that stretch across the Tyrrhenian Sea.

Parco Regionale dei Nebrodi *

Rising to the summit of Mount Soro, at a height of 1847m (5541ft), the 15 peaks of the Nebrodi Mountains now constitute a fairly new national park. The 85,680 hectare (210,000-acre) park is divided into four sections and each section has its own conservation requirements. The park is easily accessed from the *strada statale* highway along the north coast (SS113), and it has three main offices and information centres. A convenient centre is at **Alcara li Fusi** (tel: 0941 793904).

This is a very beautiful area of **unspoiled forests**, fertile pastures and abounding rivers where man has learned to live in harmony with nature. There are relatively few villages (although you will see small **stone settlements** and circular pens for the summer transhumance of livestock), and all the main centres are located on the valley roads which follow the boundaries of the park.

Botanists will find wild orchids, irises and rose peonies, while hikers may come across porcupines, foxes, ferrets, hares, snakes and plenty of green lizards. There is a chance to spot eagles, sparrowhawks and kestrels overhead, but the proliferation of deer, wild boar and wolves that once roamed this area is now history. Such creatures were hunted into extinction during the 19th and early 20th centuries.

> **THE ORIGINS OF NEBRODI**
>
> In Greek, the word *nebros* means faun, and these mountains were called thus for the proliferation of antelope that once roamed the area. Red deer and fallow deer were abundant until the 19th century, when hunting decimated their population. Today there are herds of feral black pigs, renowned for their excellent meat that is usually processed into *prosciutto* (ham).

Below: *Enigmatic ruins forming part of the Greek site at Tindari.*

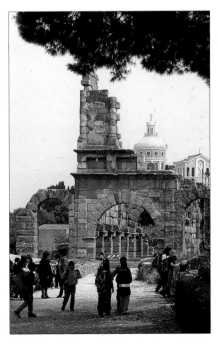

Eastern Sicily at a Glance

BEST TIMES TO VISIT

Any time is good to visit this area of Sicily, though Acireale is at its best at carnival time while Taormina has an excellent summer arts festival. This coast has a wonderful clement climate during the **autumn** and **spring**. Hotels in the cities remain open throughout the year. The **winters** can be rainy, but these days are usually followed with sunny weather. Ski enthusiasts can ski on Mount Etna's northern slopes. **Summers** are invariably hot and crowded; book ahead.

GETTING THERE

The nearest international **airport** is at **Catania**, only 5km (3 miles) from town, with direct bus links to Taormina, Messina and Milazzo. Alitalia, Air Malta, Meridiana and Lufthansa use this airport regularly. For information on flights call Catania's Fontanarossa Airport, tel: 095 349837 or 095 341654. There are also SAIS buses that link Palermo with Catania and its airport (2hr and 40min). Long-distance **bus services** transport travellers to and from Rome and Naples. Messina is the arrival point for **train** travel in Italy. It has direct connections with Catania (90min), Siracusa (3hr) and Palermo. Trains are slow, but pleasant. For all railway information in Messina (Piazza della

Repubblica), tel: 090 675234, and in Catania (Piazza Giovanni XXIII), tel: 1478 88088.

GETTING AROUND

Car rental is the easiest way to see Sicily. Avis, Hertz and Sicily by Car are all available at Catania's airport as well as in Taormina and Messina. **Bus services** link Catania and Messina (about 90min on motorway), Taormina (about 45–60min from either) and serve all points in between. From Catania, there are connections to elsewhere in Sicily. There are also buses between Palermo and Messina. For information, tel: 090 771914. In Catania, check with SAIS, tel: 095 536168, and AST, tel: 095 531756.
The Aeolian Islands are served by regular **ferry** and hydrofoil services (more during summer). There is a hydrofoil (55min) and ferry (2hr) to Lipari. For contacts see listings under Useful Contacts.

WHERE TO STAY

LUXURY
President Park Hotel, via Litteri 88, Aci Castello, tel: 095 7116111, fax: 095 277569, e-mail: htlpresident@tiscalinet.it Modern hotel, views over Ionian Sea.
Jolly Hotel, piazza Trento 13, Catania, tel: 095 316933, fax: 095 316832. A fine, central hotel with good restaurant.
Grand Hotel Timeo, via Teatro Greco 59, Taormina,

tel: 0942 23801, fax: 0942 628501. A grand hotel with a superb terrace and views.
San Domenico Palace de Taormina, piazza San Domenico 5, Taormina, tel: 0942 23701, fax: 0942 625506. Luxury hotel in former 15th-century convent.
Les Sables Noirs, Porto Ponente, Vulcano, tel: 090 9852454, fax: 090 9852454. An exclusive hideaway on this black-sanded isle.
Park Hotel La Sirenetta, via Marina 33, Stromboli, tel: 090 986025, fax: 090 986124. Modern, beachside hotel with full facilities.

MID-RANGE
Hotel Savona, via V Emanuele II 210, Catania, tel: 095 326250, fax: 095 326674. Clean and central.
Hotel del Corso, corso Umberto I 238, Taormina, tel: 0942 628698, fax: 0942 629856. A small, smart hotel in the centre of town. Some rooms have spectacular views.
Grand Hotel Liberty, via I Settembre 15, Messina, tel: 090 6409436, fax: 090 6409340, e-mail: grandhotelliberty@framon-hotels.com Central, comfortable and modern. Quality facilities.
Cincotta, Via San Pietro, Panarea, tel: 090 983014, fax: 090 983211. Delightful hotel in excellent position overlooking the sea. Good restaurant.
Hotel Signum, via Scalo 15,

Eastern Sicily at a Glance

Malfa, Salina, tel: 090 9844222, fax: 090 9844102. Pretty, local-style hotel.

Hotel Centrale Europa, via V Emanuele II 167, Catania, tel: 095 311309, fax: 095 317531. Pleasant, quiet hotel on side street of Piazza Duomo. Rooms with views.
Pensione Antea Ristorante, via Nazionale 254, Taormina Mare, Spisone, tel: 0942 24933. Clean, family-run hotel on coast. Restaurant.
Hotel Oriente, via G. Marconi 35, Lipari, tel: 090 9811493, fax: 090 9880198. Very pleasant. Quirky decoration, 300m (328yd) from port.
Residence Albergo Mendolita, Via G. Rizzo, Lipari, tel: 090 9812374, fax: 090 9812878. Self-catering. Priced according to room size.

WHERE TO EAT

LUXURY
Poggio Ducale, via Paolo Gaifami 5, Catania, tel: 095 330016. On northern side. Small hotel, fine restaurant.
La Giara, vico la Floresta 1, Taormina, tel: 0942 23360. Just off corso. One of Sicily's most highly-rated restaurants.
Piero, via Ghibellina 121, Messina, tel: 090 718365. A good restaurant in smart area.

MID-RANGE
Trattoria da Mario, via Penninello 34, Catania, 095 322461. Small, friendly and

serving Catania specialities.
Il Baccanale, piazzetta Filea 1, Taormina, tel: 0942 625390. Popular, small outside terrace with views.
Da Filippino, Via G. Rizzo, Lipari, tel: 090 9811002, e-mail: filippino@netnet.it One of Sicily's better fish restaurants. Great terrace.

BUDGET
La Piazzetta, via Paladini 5, Taormina, tel: 0942 626317. Excellent, inexpensive home cooking and local specialities.
Al Caprice, via Etnea 30–34, Catania, tel: 095 320555. Great sweets and savoury food, take out or eat in.
Trattoria Tipica Catanese, via Monte Sant'Agata 13, Catania, tel: 095 316335. Small, very typical trattoria.
Pippo Pappo, via Provinciale 214, Aci Trezza, tel: 0338 8195881. Popular fish restaurant on waterfront.

SHOPPING

Francesco Distefano, via Etnea 53, Catania, tel: 095 320745. Silversmith.
La Bottega del Buongustaio, via di Giovanni

7, Taormina, tel: 0942 625769. Specializing in home-made marzipan and *canoli*. Do not miss out on **marzipan** specialities in Taormina or Catania, and the fabulous red **pottery** from Stromboli.

USEFUL CONTACTS

Ufficio di Turismo, via Cimarosa 10, Catania, tel: 095 7306211.
Ufficio di Turismo, corso Umberto I 179, Acireale, tel: 095 604521.
Ufficio di Turismo, Piazza Sta Catarina, Taormina, tel: 0942 23243.
Ufficio di Turismo, via Calabria, isol. 301, Messina, tel: 090 674236.
Ufficio di Turismo, piazza Caio Duilio 20, Milazzo, tel: 090 9222865.
SNAV, via Rizzo 17, Milazzo, tel: 090 92877821; Siremar, via dei Mille, Milazzo, 090 9283242;
Navigazione Generale Italiana, via dei Mille 26, Milazzo, tel: 090 9284091.
Salina Diving Centre, Santa Marina Salina, Salina, tel: 0339 3503367. Arranges diving and fishing trips.

CATANIA	J	F	M	A	M	J	J	A	S	O	N	D
AVERAGE TEMP. °F	51	51	54	58	64	72	78	78	74	67	59	53
AVERAGE TEMP. °C	10	10	12	14	18	22	26	26	23	19	15	12
HOURS OF SUN DAILY	3	3	5	6	8	10	10	10	8	7	6	4
RAINFALL in	3.6	2.3	2.2	1.5	0.7	0.2	0.2	0.5	1.6	3.7	3.6	4
RAINFALL mm	91	58	56	38	18	5	5	13	41	94	91	102
DAYS OF RAINFALL	10	9	8	7	4	2	2	2	7	8	9	10

Travel Tips

Tourist Information

The government-run **Ente Nazionale Italiano per il Turismo (ENIT)** is responsible for the overseas promotion of all Italy's regions. Their offices can be found: in the UK at 1 Princes Street, London WIR 8AY, tel: 020 7408 1254, fax: 020 7493 6695; in the USA at 500 N Michigan Ave, Suite 2240, Chicago I, Illinois 60611, tel: 321 664 0996, fax: 312 644 3019, or 630 Fifth Ave, Suite 1565, New York, NY 10111, tel: 212 245 4822, fax: 212 586 9249, and 124000 Wilshire Blvd, Suite 550, Los Angeles, CA 90025, tel: 310 820 1959, fax: 310 820 6357.

Within Sicily, each province handles its own tourism promotion through its individual **Azienda Autonoma Provinciale per l'Incremento Turistico (AAPIT)**, located in the capital of each province. The Regione Siciliana Assessorato Turismo is at via Notarbartolo 11, Palermo, tel: 091 6968032. For information go to website: www.aapit.pa.it and www.sicily.go.com

Entry Requirements

To enter Italy, EU visitors require a national identity card or a **passport**, valid for six months after the date of arrival. All other visitors require a valid passport. For visits over 90 days, a visa is necessary. Drivers need an international licence (domestic licences for EU nationals), the car's documents and Green Card, providing insurance.

Customs

Custom regulations for EU citizens are 800 cigarettes, 200 cigars or 1kg (2.2lb) tobacco; 10 litres (about 16 pints) spirits, 90 litres (about 120 bottles) wine and 100 litres (160 pints) of beer. For non-EU nationals, the limits are 400 cigarettes, 100 cigars, 1 litre spirits or 2 litres wine.

Health Requirements

There are no specific health requirements; refer to health precautions on page 126.

Getting There

By air: The principal airport, Falcone Borsellino Airport (tel: 091 6019111 for domestic flights and tel: 091 591275 for international flights), is outside **Palermo**, located 30km (19 miles) west of the city. The other airport is Fontanarossa Airport (tel: 095 349837 or 095 341654) at **Catania**, located just 4km (2.5 miles) to the south of the city. Both airports receive scheduled and charter flights. Visitors from North America can fly to Sicily via Milan or Rome with a plane change. Bus services link Palermo's airport (tel: 091 586351) and Catania's airport (tel: 095 536170) to the centre of town. Etna Transporti ensures transport between these airports and other towns throughout Sicily.

By rail: the Ferrovie dello Stato (Italian State Railway) has first- and second-class services from Palermo, Catania and Siracusa right through to Naples (6–7hr), Rome (8–9hr) and Milan (12–14hr). Sleeper services are available on the longer routes. For railway details (in English): www.fs-on-line.com or in Sicily (in Italian): tel: 1478 88088.

By road: Once across the Strait Messina it is beneficial to have one's own car, though foreign cars are targets for theft, so take care. Frequent car ferries cross these Straits, between Reggio di Calabria and Messina, in less than 45min. Milan is a 1260km (788 miles), Rome is 685km (429 miles) and Naples about 480km (300 miles) from Messina.

By sea: There are regular ferries from either Genoa (20hr), Livorno (17hr) or Naples (11hr) to Palermo, or from Naples to Milazzo. Adventurous travellers can continue to Valletta Malta (details from Island Seaway, Molo Centrale Porto, Siracusa, tel: 095 325081, or Virtu Ferries, Agenzia La Duca Viaggi, tel: 095 316711) or to Tunis (details from Trapani, tel: 1478 99000). Information for national departures from Grimaldi-Grandi Navi Veloci, Calata Marinai d'Italia, Palermo, tel: 091 587404, fax: 091 6110088, or Tirrenia Navigazione, Calata Marinai d'Italia, Palermo, tel: 1478 990000, fax: 091 6021221.

What to Pack

Bring warm clothing, an umbrella and a rain jacket during the winter months. Spring and autumn are often warm so a range of suitable clothing is the best option. Summer clothing should be light and a hat is a good idea. Most restaurants do not require tie and jacket, but since Italians love dressing up, one should make an effort.

GOOD READING

Gefen, Gerard, *Sicilian Twilight*, Vendome Press, 2001
Homer, *The Odyssey*, translated by Martin Hammond, published by Duckworth, 2000
Lampedusa, Giuseppe Tommasi de, *The Leopard*, translated by Archibald Colquhoun, Harvill Press, 1996
Phelps, Daphne, *A House in Sicily*, Virago, 2000
Pirandello, Luigi, *Six Characters in Search of an Author*, translated by Mark Musa, Penguin Books Australia, 1995
Puzo, Mario, *The Sicilian*, Arrow Books, 2000
Runciman, Steven, *Sicilian Vespers*, Cambridge University Press, 1992
Suscsia, Leonardo, *Sicilian Uncles*, Carcanet Press, 1986
Simeti, Mary Taylor, *On Persephone's Island*, Vintage, 1995, and *Pomp and Sustenance: 25 Centuries of Sicilian Food*, Ebury Press, 1991
Sontag, Susan, *The Volcano Lover*, Farrar, Strauss & Giroux, 1992; or Anchor Books, 1993
Sterling, Claire, *The Mafia*, Harper Collins, 1991
Verga, Giovanni, *Cavalleria Rusticana and Other Stories*, translated by Harry McWilliam, Penguin, 1999

Bring good footwear and binoculars for those badly lit churches. Pack a separate purse for the change required to light chapels and churches.

Money Matters

Italy is one of the 12 members of the European Union and the currency is now the Euro. The fixed rate is 1936.27 lire. The south of Italy is supposed to be less expensive than the north, but this depends on where you go in Sicily. If you are travelling in the rural areas or in smaller towns, it is advisable to take cash, as cheques and credit cards are not always accepted. To exchange money use an exchange office where you see the sign *cambio*, as the service is far simpler than that of a bank. They are quicker, although they do take a substantial percentage. An ATM, called a **Bancomat**, is the easiest way to obtain currency with your credit card.

Accommodation

There is a range of accommodation to suit most budgets and a star-rating system distinguishes the hotels. Italy is fairly expensive and Sicily is no exception. The top-of-the-range, luxury *alberghi* hotels can be as expensive as those in Rome. However, there is plenty of accommodation in the mid-range category. *Agriturismo* (accommodation in the countryside) is a growing sector of the hospitality business. It can be exceptionally pleasant and very comfortable; website: www.agriturismo.regione. sicilia.it *Pensioni* are a good option and some of them are quite luxurious. At the bottom of the budget are very basic *Residenze*. If your hotel is on the outskirts, the price is more affordable. The approximate costs of a double bedroom are calculated as follows:
Budget: 45 to 75 Euros (bathrooms may be shared)

Mid-range: 80 to 110 Euros
Luxury: 115 to 200 Euros or
230,000 to 400,000 lire.
Hotels with rooms costing
over 200 Euros are
mentioned as deluxe.

Eating Out

Each region has its own
specialities along with other
Italian favourites. *Ristoranti*
(with good menus and expansive wine lists) are the most
expensive, while the *trattorie*
may not be as pricey. For less
expensive options try a *tavola
calda* or a *pizzeria* (some sell
pizza slices for takeaway
consumption). Many city
restaurants close in August,
and once or twice in the
week, while resort restaurants
often close out of season.
For a fine meal, without wine,
at a restaurant in the **Luxury**
category, expect to pay over
50 Euros. At a **mid-range**
restaurant, between 30 and
45 Euros and for a **budget**
meal, less than 25 Euros.

Transport

Air: There is no air transport
within Sicily except for
services between Palermo and

Trapani, Lampedusa or
Pantelleria. There are also
direct flights between Italian
towns and Sicily in summer.
Rail: the railway operated by
the Ferrovie dello Stato (State
Railways) links many Sicilian
towns. Contact the organiza-
tion in Palermo at Stazione
Centrale, tel: 1478 88088.
Details on the railway services
can be found (in English) at
www.fs-on-line.com
Bus: The intercity bus services
are very good, especially
between the larger towns.
The main bus services are
operated by AST (tel: 091
6882783 or 091 6882906),
SAIS Autolinee (tel: 091
6166028) and SEGESTA (tel:
091 61167919). Local orange
buses ply the streets of all
major towns. Tickets are flat
fares valid for 90min.
Car: Taxis are freely available.
Car rental is available at the
airports and in the centres of
Palermo, Catania, Messina,
Siracusa and Trapani.
Although transactions are
secured when paid prior to
your arrival, the following
companies (listed in Palermo)
are on the island: Avis, via E

Amari 91, tel: 091 586940;
Sixt, via A Casella 66, tel: 167
163333; Hertz Italiana, via
Messina 7/e, tel: 091 331668;
Maggiore, via A de Gasperi
79, tel: 091 517305, and
Sicily by Car, via M Stabile 6/a,
tel: 091 581045.
The roads are generally good,
but those in the mountainous
areas are not as well maintained. The *autostrade* are
toll-paying motorways.
Bear in mind that driving in
Palermo and Catania is chao-
tic, so try to avoid rush hours.
Note that all drivers must
carry their driver's licences,
wear seat belts and shoes
while driving and have a red
warning triangle in case of an
accident/breakdown. Speed
limits are 110kph (68mph) on
major roads and 130kph
(81mph) on the *autostrade*.
On-the-spot fines are usually
given to speeding drivers.
An anti-theft steering-wheel
lock is an effective deterrent
against car theft.
Carriage: Sicily still has some
horse-drawn carriages. They
are not cheap, but a pleasant
way to explore.
Boat: Boat services are many.
Apart from the services connecting Sicily to mainland Italy
and Corsica, Malta and
Tunisia, there are frequent
services to the Aeolian Islands
from Milazzo (contacts: SNAV,
via Rizzo 17, Milazzo, tel: 090
92877821; Siremar, Via dei
Mille, Milazzo, 090 9283242;
Navigazione Generale Italiana,
via dei Mille 26, Milazzo, tel:
090 9284091), from Palermo
(SNAV, via Belmonte 55,
tel: 091 333333 or 091

CONVERSION CHART		
FROM	**TO**	**MULTIPLY BY**
Millimetres	Inches	0.0394
Metres	Yards	1.0936
Metres	Feet	3.281
Kilometres	Miles	0.6214
Square kilometres	Square miles	0.386
Hectares	Acres	2.471
Litres	Pints	1.760
Kilograms	Pounds	2.205
Tonnes	Tons	0.984
To convert Celsius to Fahrenheit: x 9 ÷ 5 + 32		

6118525; Siremar, via F Crispi 118, tel: 091 582403) and seasonal services from Cefalù (contact: SNAV, corso Ruggero 76, tel: 0921 421050).
For travel to Ustica from Palermo, contact Siremar, via Crispi 120, Palermo, tel: 091-336631 and to the Egadi Islands from Trapani contact Siremar, via Staiti 61/63, tel: 0923 540515. There are also ferry services between Messina (contacts: SNAV, via San Raineri 22, tel: 090 7775; Società Caronte Shipping, rada San Francesco, tel: 090 52966) and Villa San Giovanni or Reggio di Calabria. Journeys take between 15 and 35 minutes.

Business Hours

Food shops and markets:
These open around 07:30, closing for lunch from around 12:30 to 13:00. Shops reopen in the afternoon at around 16:00 until 19:00 or later.
Banks: Banks are open Monday to Friday from 08:30 to 13:30 and again from 14:30 to 15:30. They are closed over the weekends. They also close earlier prior to a public holiday. Using ATM outlets saves time and offers the possibility to obtain cash 24 hours a day.
Museums and Monuments:
The hours are generally as follows: open from Tuesday through to Saturday, from 9:00 to 19:00, with a two-hour lunch break, and Sundays from 9:00 to 13:00. Archaeological sites are usually open each day from early

morning to sunset.
In the text we have used the terms 'morning' and 'after-noon' as the venue is closed over lunch (any time between 12:00 and 15:00) and 'daily' means that it is open from morning to late afternoon, unless otherwise stated.
Churches: These open in the early morning at around 7:00 and close at 18:00. Most churches will close over lunch (between 12:00 and 16:00).

Time Difference

Italy's time is GMT plus one hour in winter and GMT plus two hours in summer. Thus when it is 12 noon in London on a December day, it is 13:00 in Sicily. The 24-hour clock is used.

Communications

Post: The mail service can be slow in summer with the influx of tourist mail. Stamps for postcards and letters can be bought from

ROAD SIGNS
Senso unico • One-way street
Alt • Stop and *Avanti* • Go
Sottopassaggio • Pedestrian underpass
Passo carribile • Entrance constantly in use
Benzina • Petrol/gas
Fermata • Bus stop
Divieto di sosta • No stopping
Uscita • Exit
Questura • Police station
Autostrada • Motorway
Pedaggio • Toll
Accendere i fari • Turn on lights
Curva molto pericolosa • Very dangerous bend

Tabacchi (tobacconists) – longer hours than *La Posta* (the post office). For packages and other mail go to the Ufficio Postale Centrale (the main post office) in Palermo at via Roma 322, open Monday to Friday from 08:10 to 19:25 and on Saturdays it closes over lunchtime. In Catania it is at via Etnea 215.
Telephones: Public phones are found on streets, at post offices and in bars and restaurants. These are operated by coins and prepaid *schede* or *carte telephoniche*, (telephone cards) which are available at newsstands, post offices or *tabacchi*. Some telephone cabins accept credit cards and others send faxes.
Italy offers Home Direct dialling and various toll-free numbers will link you with AT&T, MCI, Telstra, British Telecom, One-Tel and other international systems for debiting your home account. All numbers in Italy start with a 0 unless they are free. You must always dial the 0 and the code whether you are in the same town or overseas. Palermo's code is 091; Catania's is 095; Agrigento's is 0922 and Siracusa's is 0931. All are followed by the subscriber's number.
To dial out of the country, dial 00 followed by the country's code and then the city or area code, without the 0 before it, and the subscriber's number. If dialling TO Italy from over-seas, you need to dial the 0 of the code.
Faxes: These can be sent from post offices and a num-

ber of cabins in major towns.
Internet: Only some hotels permit the use of this. Cyber cafés are found in Palermo, Siracusa and Catania.

Electricity

The current is 220V AC, plugs are two pinned and adapters are available in electrical stores and airports.

Weights and Measures

Italy follows the metric system. Food (such as slices of cold meats, pâtés and fruits) is often sold by the *etto*, which is 100g (3.4oz).

Health Precautions

There are no particular health warnings. The tap water is safe and bottled mineral water is widely available. In summer, one should have sunscreen and mosquito repellent. Medical facilities are good, but expensive. Make sure you take out medical insurance. If you come from an EU country, you are eligible for free emergency medical care under EU regulations and require Form E111. Obtain and validate one from your local post office before leaving home. You may receive first aid (*pronto soccorso*) at the outpatients department of the local hospital, the railway station and the airport, or dial **113**.

Personal Safety

Petty theft and car theft is rife, so do not tempt chance. Keep all your valuables out of sight and leave your passports and airline tickets in your hotel. Carry money and credit cards in a money belt. Never leave anything visible in your car. Rather pay for your parking than take the risk of leaving your car in a back street. Women are advised not to walk alone late at night. Do not worry about the Mafia, as it is very unlikely that the visitor will have any contact with them.

Emergencies

If robbed, report the incident to the *carabinieri* (military police), tel: **113** (at their *caserma*) or to the *polizia* (civil police) at the *questura*. For fire emergencies, tel: **115** and for emergency assistance on the road, tel: **116**. For health emergencies, tel: **118.**

Etiquette

Sicily is reputedly more traditional than the rest of Italy. Out of town, decorous dress and courtesy is the rule and swimwear, skimpy shorts and T-shirts are not permitted in churches. Topless sunbathing is still outlawed. Many urban Sicilians speak a little English; if you do not speak Italian, a *buon giorno*, *grazie* and *arrivederci* are always appreciated along with a handshake and a polite *piacere*.

Tipping

More expensive restaurants add an automatic 10–15 per cent on to the bill. The rest rely on the client's benevolence. There is no obligation to give tips and it may be at your own discretion. Italians leave a reasonable gratuity and tourists usually leave no tip or far too much.

Language

Apart from the national language, most Italians involved in the tourist industry also speak English and French.

USEFUL PHRASES
Good day • *Buon giorno*
Good evening • *Buona sera*
Hi or Bye • *Ciao*
Goodbye • *Arrivederci*
Please • *Per piacere*
Thank you • *Grazie*
Okay • *D'accordo*
Excuse me • *Mi scusi*
I'm sorry • *Mi dispiace*
How are you? • *Come sta?*
Fine, thanks • *Bene, grazie*
Help • *Aiuto*
I do not feel well • *Non mi sento bene*
Please call a doctor • *Chiami un medico per favore*
What time does it open? • *A che ora apre?*
Where is? • *Dov'è?*
What time is it? • *Che ora è?* (or in the afternoon: *Che ora sono?*)
Do you speak English? French? • *Parla Inglese? Francese?*
I don't understand • *Non capisco*
Please speak slowly • *Parli più lentamente per favore*
Open • *Aperto*
Closed • *Chiuso*
How much does this cost? • *Quanto costa questo?*
Post office • *L'ufficio postale*
Grocer's • *Gli alimentari*
Baker's • *Il panificio*
Greengrocer's • *Il fruttaiolo*
Pharmacy • *La farmacia*
Book store • *La libreria*
Library • *La biblioteca*
Pastry shop • *La pasticceria*
Municipality • *Comune*

INDEX